British Buses, Trams and Trolleybuses 1950s-1970s

British Buses, Trams and Trolleybuses 1950s-1970s

The operators and their vehicles

Part 10: Midland Independent Operators

Henry Conn

SLP

Silver Link Publishing Ltd

First published in 2013

British Library Cataloguing in Publication Data

A catalogue record for this book is available from the British Library.

ISBN 978 1 85794 425 9

Silver Link Publishing Ltd
The Trundle
Ringstead Road
Great Addington
Kettering
Northants NN14 4BW

Tel/Fax: 01536 330588
email: sales@nostalgiacollection.com
Website: www.nostalgiacollection.com
Printed and bound in the Czech Republic

Any photographs not otherwise credited were taken by the author or are from his collection.

Title page: **MRR 974 was an all-Leyland PSU1/11 new to South Notts in March 1952, and is seen here passing Trent Bridge, Nottingham, on a journey to Thrumpton.** *Mark Hampson collection*

Acknowledgements

Some of the photographs within this book have come from my collection, but my most sincere thanks go to Brian Botley and Mark Hampson for access to their excellent collections of negatives and slides, many of which can be seen in this volume. Many thanks also to Nigel Chevin-Hall and Glen Bubb for their very much appreciated assistance in PSV publications for the areas covered in this volume.

The PSV publications dealing with all the operators illustrated, and many early issues of *Buses Illustrated*, were vital sources of information for this book.

Contents

Introduction   6
Astill & Jordan   8
Austin's (Woodseaves)   9
Barton Transport   13
Berresfords Motors   27
Blue Bus Services (Tailby & George)   33
Charlton-on-Otmoor Services   38
Chiltern Queens   42
W. Gash & Sons (Newark)   46
Green Bus Company   50
Harper Brothers (Heath Hayes)   54
House's (Watlington)   59
Hulley's (Baslow)   60
Hylton & Dawson (Glenfield)   66
F. Procter & Sons (Hanley)   67
Red Rover (Aylesbury)   69
Shropshire independents   72
Silver Service (Darley Dale)   94
Skill's (Nottingham)   98
South Notts   100
J. Stevenson (Uttoxeter)   106
W. Stonier & Sons   110
S. Turner & Sons (Brown Edge)   116
Warrington (Ilam)   117
Warstone Motors (Green Bus Service)   118
E. Webster & Sons (Hognaston)   122
Worth's Motor Services (Enstone)   123
York Brothers (Northampton)   124

Introduction

In the first of my *British Buses, Trams and Trolleybus* volumes, which dealt with the Midlands, there was very little room to cover the large number of independent operators in the area, so this volume fills that gap.

The Green Bus Company provided services from Uttoxeter to Lichfield and Hednesford, and these were later extended to Cannock and Rugeley.

In the late 1960s Harper Brothers of Heath Hayes had a fleet of around 50 buses, which included ex-London Transport RTLs, an assortment of Leyland Titans bought new, and Daimler Fleetlines. The main service was from Heath Hayes through Brownhills to Aldridge.

Vaggs of Knockin Heath operated rural services and had a route between Oswestry and Shrewsbury. The company's fleet in the late 1960s was a varied assortment of Bedfords, Bristol SCs and Leylands, together with a couple of ex-City of Oxford AEC Regents. Local services in or around Oswestry were provided by Hampson's, which for a number of years used two ex-London AEC Regal IVs. Salopia Saloon Coaches provided a service between Whitchurch and Shrewsbury with a Willowbrook-bodied Bedford. There were also a number of small operators providing services in the Shrewsbury area, and a number were members of the Shropshire Omnibus Owners Association, including Brown's of Donnington Wood, which ran Sentinels in regular services until 1974.

The biggest independent in the Potteries area was Berresfords Motors of Cheddleton, which served the Leek, Hanley and Longton areas. The company's 30-strong bus fleet included 25-year-old Leyland Titans, many of which were acquired from Stockport Corporation, and an ex-Silver Star Leyland PDR1/1.

Also serving Leek was Procter & Sons of Hanley, which had a smaller fleet than Berresfords, but almost all its buses were purchased new.

Stonier's of Goldenhill ran a service between Hanley and Bentilee jointly with Potteries Motor Traction, using a fleet made up mainly of Leyland PD2s and PD3s.

Turner of Brown Edge operated a service to Hanley using Leyland PDs and PD3s together with Northern Counties-bodied Daimler CRGs purchased new.

Stevenson's of Uttoxeter ran a service to Burton-upon-Trent and from there to Ashbourne, operating a fleet of around 40 buses of very mixed makes. They came from a number of operators and included London Transport, City of Oxford, Portsmouth, Sheffield and Yorkshire Traction.

Blue Bus Services ran services between Derby and Burton using a fleet predominantly made up of Daimlers. All the company's double-deckers were of lowheight or lowbridge design and included a couple of Dennis Lolines. Unfortunately, in January 1976 19 buses and coaches were destroyed by fire at the Blue Bus depot at Willington, and only one Daimler CVG6 and a Dennis Loline survived from the company's fleet.

Silver Service of Darley Dale ran a number of services from Matlock using a number of assorted second-hand buses, such as a pair of Doncaster AEC Reliances, but also one or two buses purchased new, which included 1965 Strachan-bodied Bedfords.

A number of independent operators operated regular services into Nottingham.

The smallest was Skill's, using Leyland PD3s on a route between Nottingham and East Bridgford. The largest was Barton Transport, whose fleet in the late 1960s was more than 300 strong, based at Chilwell, and covered Nottingham, Leicester, Derby, Ilkeston and Long Eaton. In the 1950s and 1960s Barton had purchased a plethora of new and used buses, and in the same period had rebuilt a number of old buses to extend their service lives. The amazing variety of new, second-hand and rebuilt buses are covered in this volume.

South Notts, whose depot was in Gotham, operated services to Clifton and Loughborough, run mainly by double-deck buses. In 1970 there were 24 double-deckers in service, ranging from Leyland PD2s to Leyland PD3s, Albion Lowlanders, Leyland Atlanteans and Daimler Fleetlines. One of the Lowlanders purchased new in 1967 was the last to be built.

Gash of Newark also operated into Nottingham and had a number of services around Newark. In 1970 Gash ran a fleet of around 20 buses and 10 coaches, of which eight were Daimler CVD6s and a 1954 Daimler CVG6; until 1979 this bus was the most modern double-decker in the fleet.

Small service operators in the Leicester area included Astill & Jordan of Ratby, with an ex-Leicester Leyland PD3, and Hylton & Dawson of Glenfield.

York Brothers of Northampton provided a local service in Northampton and had a small fleet of very well turned-out coaches.

A service to Oxford was provided by Charlton-on-Otmoor Services using ex-South Wales AEC Regent Vs, ex-London Transport AEC Regents or second-hand AEC Reliances. Also running in City of Oxford territory was Chiltern Queens of Woodcote, with services in the Wallingford area and running to Reading; the fleet was predominantly made up of AEC Reliances.

Worth's of Enstone also ran a service to Oxford, and also used second-hand AEC Reliances.

Red Rover of Aylesbury ran local services in Aylesbury with new and second-hand AEC buses including Regents, two Bridgemasters, a Renown, Reliances and a couple of Swifts.

Enjoy the nostalgia!

Chiltern Queens of Woodcote, Oxfordshire, purchased three Duple bus-bodied AEC Reliances, LMO 743 to 745, which were delivered in 1955. This view of LMO 744 was taken at Reading railway station in 1968. *Brian Botley*

Astill & Jordan

The business was started in 1920 by Stinson Astill with a little financial backing from M. Jordan. The first vehicle to be purchased was a left-hand-drive Traffic delivery van, which was fitted with seats. The original route was Ratby, Kirby Corner, Bloods Hill, Braunstone Cross Roads and along Hinckley Road, terminating at the 'Sailor's Return' in Leicester. After 1930 the service was altered to run through Glenfield, and from there was worked jointly with another old established operator, Hylton & Dawson. During the post-war boom the business expanded its operations into private hire and works and school contracts. The stage service into Leicester now terminated at St Margaret's bus station. The business became a limited company in 1962.

In 1956 the business decided to operate double-deck buses on the main Leicester service; four Leyland TD5s were acquired, and their success paved the way for further second-hand double-deckers. AEC Regent III LUC 443, seen in St Margaret's bus station in September 1964, is former London Transport RT 4094, which entered service from Harrow Weald depot in April 1951. It was transferred to New Cross in January 1957 and stayed there until overhaul at Aldenham in January 1959, when the original Weymann body was removed and replaced with a Park Royal roofbox body. The bus then passed to Holloway depot, where it stayed until put into store in April 1964, being purchased by Astill & Jordan in June. On the left is HKR 42, one of three Weymann-bodied Bristol K6As new to Maidstone & District in 1947 and purchased in the early 1960s. *Brian Botley*

Double-deck operations ceased in 1968, but the building of a large housing estate in Ratby and large new County Council offices in Glenfield reversed the downward trend in passenger numbers and it was found necessary to start double-decker operations again. In 1978 the company acquired Leicester Corporation's 82 HBC, an East Lancashire-bodied Leyland PD3A/1 new in 1964. Platform doors and moquette seating were fitted before the bus entered service, and this view of it, looking very smart, was taken at St Margaret's bus station in May 1979. *Mark Hampson collection*

Austin's (Woodseaves)

G. H. Austin & Son Ltd of Woodseaves, Staffordshire, was founded in 1927 by W. H. Austin, and the first service operated was from a garage at Knightley Gorse, between Stafford and Newport. The coach business started from what was originally a coal merchant's operation; at weekends the coach was cleaned, furnished with seats and used for day trips.

In October 1936 R. Edwards of Newport and of G. B. Williams of Eaton-on-Tern were acquired, followed in January 1938 by the business of R. A. Layton of Cannock. Around the same time the fleet size increased rapidly with the acquisition of the business of R. Beard of Newport, and by 1942 it had grown to almost 50 buses.

Just after the end of the war Austin's acquired Station Garage, Derby Street, Stafford, from Worthington Motor Tours Ltd. In December 1950 the stage services of A. R. Morris of Bridgnorth were acquired, followed just over five years later by E. Jones of Shifnal. By 1961 Austin's had four operational garages, at Woodseaves, Cannock, Stafford and Newport. However, in October 1963 the Cannock business was sold, only the garage being retained and converted to a car salesroom, then in 1964 the Stafford garage was closed and also converted to car showrooms. In July 1969 a receiver was appointed to run the business, and in April 1971 a new company, Happy Days (Woodseaves) Limited, emerged.

During 1935 Todmorden Corporation purchased two all-Leyland TD4s, Nos 37 and 38 (AWU 664 and 665), and they lasted in service until 1948. No 37 was acquired by Austin's and during 1952 received a Beadle L26/26R body. During September 1957 the bus was again re-bodied with a rare Auto Cellulose (Spon Lane, Smethwick) coach body and numbered 55. This is AWU 664 in the spring of 1960, just before its withdrawal from service in July of that year. *Brian Botley*

During 1955 Smith's and Webster's of Wigan purchased a number of Leyland PSUC1/2s with Alexander coach bodywork, and between December 1957 and March 1958 Austin's purchased one from Webster (BJP 388) and two from Smith (BJP 272 and BJP 273). Heading for Gnosall in the summer of 1964 is BJP 273, which remained in the fleet until December 1971. *Brian Botley*

In 1956 Duple purchased a Leyland PSUC1/2, 103 KMM, and it received a Duple Donington C41F body for demonstration purposes. The bus was later purchased by Hall Brothers of South Shields, then in November 1964 Austin's purchased it from Harding of Birkenhead, and it is seen here taking passengers for the service to Newport in the summer of 1965. The bus remained in the Austin's fleet until October 1968. *Brian Botley*

Skill's of Nottingham purchased a dual-purpose Willowbrook-bodied Leyland Royal Tiger, OTO 63, in 1952, and in December of 1963 this bus was acquired by Austin's. The first photograph was taken in early 1964 and shows the bus still in Skill's livery; the second view shows the Austin's livery in the summer of 1965. The bus remained with Austin's until July 1967 and was later noted with Aston of Marton in October 1967. *Mark Hampson collection/Brian Botley*

During the 1960s Austin's purchased a number of Leyland Tiger Cubs for work on the company's country bus services to the west of Stafford. Most of these had Weymann bus bodywork and were acquired from Western Welsh. The first view, taken in the summer of 1971, shows JBO 63 and JBO 85, which were both new to Western Welsh in 1954. In the other picture is JBO 87, heading for Newport in August 1969. *Mark Hampson collection/ Brian Botley*

The Bedford SB was the first Bedford vehicle to have a 'forward control' design, with the driver's seat located to the right of the engine and the front axle underneath. It used a four-speed synchromesh gearbox (five-speed boxes were offered later), and could be fitted with Bedford's own petrol or diesel engine, with the Perkins R6 and Leyland O.350 and O.370 engines also being

offered during the 1950s and 1960s. Austin's purchased three Duple-bodied Bedford SB5s (VBF 2 to 4) new in 1962, and representing this batch in July 1965 is the first of them. A new Bedford SB5 had a Bedford 5.42-litre diesel engine fitted. *Brian Botley*

Barton Transport

Barton No 349 (EVO 713) was one of four Leyland TD5s delivered in 1939 with Duple L27/26F bodies, which were the forerunners of the large fleet of Duple-bodied Leyland PD1s delivered after the war. The entrance is set back from the front bulkhead to allow the staircase to be fitted running across the width of the bus and leading to the sunken gangway that went to the rear from the bulkhead. There was a step up to the left of the front seat to give the driver full headroom in his cab. This view was taken just a short time before the withdrawal of the bus from the fleet in the summer of 1959. *Brian Botley*

Above: **During 1952 Barton purchased a number of Roe-bodied Leyland TD5s from Leeds Corporation, and one of them, No 682 (FNW 702), is seen in Nottingham in September 1959 about to take up a journey to Epperstone.** *Brian Botley*

Below: **This is No 951 (JAT 410), a Roe-bodied Leyland PD1 new to East Yorkshire in 1949. This moody view was taken in the winter of 1962.** *Brian Botley*

Right: **The Ministry of War Transport authorised the recommencement of bus production in late 1941. The specification was for a very basic timber-framed body, steel panelling and a minimum of panel-beaten curved surfaces; initially it provided for only one opening window per side per deck, and a steel-panelled emergency 'window' at the back. From mid-1943 wooden slatted seats were specified, then in late 1944 aluminium panelling was allowed, as were panel-beaten roof domes, more opening windows and a reversion to upholstered seats; however, these relaxations did not generally come into effect until mid-1945. The MoWT specification for lowbridge bodies provided for 28 passengers on the lower deck and 27 on the upper deck, the lower deck being provided with six pairs of transverse two-seaters and longitudinal two-seaters over the wheel arch, although some bodies, typically early Strachan versions, had five pairs of transverse seats and four-seaters over the wheel arch. This is Barton No 443 (GNN 704), a Strachan Utility-bodied Guy Arab II new in 1945. I believe that**

this bus was fitted with platform doors in 1954/55 and this view was taken in Melton Mowbray bus station in July 1960. *Brian Botley*

Below: A large number of Duple lowheight-bodied Leyland PD1s were purchased new by Barton in 1947 and 1948. Numerically the first was No 453 (JNN 793), seen here standing at Huntingdon Street bus station, Nottingham, in September 1965. The next bus in line is No 722 (RAL 37), a Plaxton-bodied Leyland BTS/1 new to Barton in 1953. The South Notts bus on the left is one of the company's Northern Counties-bodied Albion Lowlander LR3s. *Brian Botley*

Above: **There was only one mass-produced derivative of the PS1, which was the coach variant with a drop-frame extension for a luggage boot. This was coded PS1/1, and was a very strong seller, forming the major post-war fleet renewals for large UK coach firms such as Southdown, Ribble, Wallace Arnold, Grey Green and Barton. A number of Duple-bodied Leyland PS1/1s were purchased new** by Barton in 1948, and standing at Melton Mowbray bus station in July 1958 is No 559 (KAL 204). *Brian Botley*

Below: **Four Leyland BTS1/1s with Barton's own bodywork entered service in 1952, numbered 596 to 599 (NNN 80 to 82 and NNN 967). This is No 597 (NNN 81) in Nottingham in October 1958.** *Brian Botley*

Above: **Standing in a quiet street in Nottingham in October 1958 is No 724 (RAL 39), a Leyland BTS/1 with Plaxton coachwork new in 1953.** *Brian Botley*

Below: **In June 1950 there was a further revision to the construction and use regulations, and buses 8-foot wide no longer required special permission, while the maximum length for double-deck buses was increased to 27 feet. As a result Leyland raised a new set of variant codes for the PD2,** with a wheelbase of 16ft 5in. The standard Leyland body was also revised. The new type codes for the Titan were PD2/10 (7ft 6 in wide, vacuum brakes); PD2/11 (7ft 6in wide, air brakes); PD2/12 (8 feet wide, vacuum brakes); and PD2/13 (8 feet wide, air brakes). Barton purchased two all-Leyland PD2/12s in 1953, Nos 731 and 732 (RAL 333 and 334), and seen at Huntingdon Street bus station in November 1969 is No 732 (RAL 334). *Mark Hampson collection*

Right: **About to work a service from Melton Mowbray to Bingham in October 1958 is No 744 (SRR 776), a Plaxton Venturer coach-bodied AEC Reliance new to Barton in 1954. The Venturer combined the front of the Crusader with more restrained and conservative styling, and proved so popular that it was not long before a version was produced for front-engined chassis, mostly lightweight Bedfords and Commers, with a rather more raked frontal appearance. By the time the Mark II version appeared at the 1952 Commercial Motor Show, the Venturer was Plaxton's standard model. The Venturer II had a common front profile for all models, together with a standard dash panel featuring a four-part radiator grille with an oval outline and a central cross, which also embraced the headlamps. A rear-end revision marked the launch of the Venturer III in 1954, and the following year a version was produced for underfloor-engined chassis with the entrance ahead of the front axle. This required a return to a more vertical front profile, and meant that there were now three variants of the Venturer: front-engined, underfloor-engined with a centre entrance, and underfloor-engined with a front entrance.** *Brian Botley*

Right: **During 1957 Barton purchased two Duple-bodied AEC Reliances from Creamline of Borden, and they** were given fleet numbers 771 and 772 (OCG 9 and NOR 511). This is the second of them in Nottingham in September 1966. The parked car in the background is a Ford Zodiac Mark III. The Zodiac was an upmarket version of the Zephyr 6, but differed considerably from that model by the limousine-type rear doors, sharper roofline (with narrower C-pillar) and tail, unique grille (four headlights instead of two), exclusive bumper bars, plusher seating, and upmarket upholstery, dashboard and interior fittings. *Mark Hampson collection*

Right: The ninth-built AEC Reliance, registered MHO 362, was new to Creamline of Borden in 1954 and had Mann Egerton coach bodywork. That company was better known as a Norwich motor car dealer, although it bodied many early post-war Austins and small coaches; however, it also built bodywork for larger coaches and a very few double-deck buses. This view of No 778 was taken in August 1968. On the extreme right is the front of a 1967 Vauxhall Viva, and beyond it the front of a Riley/Sunbeam 1500, then a Standard Ten, a Skoda and a Rover. *Mark Hampson collection*

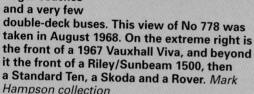

Below: Like a number of companies in the 1950s, Barton rebuilt a number of Leyland PS1/1 Tigers, some of which received double-deck bodies by Willowbrook. This is No 781 (WAL 781), which was new to Barton in 1948 as a Leyland PS1/1 saloon and was rebuilt in 1957. To the right are two of the Duple-bodied Leyland PD1s that were new in 1948, and on the left is No 820 (PDD 978), which had been new to Marchant of Cheltenham in 1955 and was purchased by Barton in 1959. This view was taken at Melton Mowbray in September 1959. *Brian Botley*

Above Standing at Broad Marsh, Nottingham, in May 1959 is one of the Leyland PS1/1s rebuilt with Northern Counties bodywork, new in 1958. Seven were built in 1959, and representing this batch is No 797 (797 BAL). In the background, working for Nottingham Tyre Services, is a Ford Thames 400E, which all in all was a good van, and well suited too many uses, although some may well think otherwise if they had one late in its life. If well maintained, the 400E could put up a very lively performance, often being first away from the lights, and for deliveries it was most useful, especially with the nearside door to get at the load. It was also very easy to slip over the offside wheel arch down to the ground in one step when making your exit from the cab. *Brian Botley*

Below: During July 1959 Barton took delivery of No 825 (70 DNN), a Harrington-bodied AEC Reliance. Standing behind it in this September 1961 view is No 815 (815 CNN), a Duple-bodied Ford Thames Trader that was new to Barton in 1959. *Brian Botley*

Above: During 1946 Leicester City Corporation took delivery of 20 all-Leyland PD1s, and by the end of 1959 Barton had purchased 14 of them. Standing at Long Eaton depot in the summer of 1971 is No 844 (DJF 339). *Mark Hampson collection*

Below: For lightweight chassis, such as the Bedford or Ford Thames, the new Burlingham design was to be known as the Seagull 60, the first time that the Seagull name had been officially applied to a design for front-engined vehicles. Sales of the Seagull 60 were good, but the body type did have a flaw in the form of a raised Perspex section in the centre of the roof, which ran all the way from front to rear, which admitted rainwater due to inadequate rubber sealing, although this could be corrected at considerable expense. This is Barton No 911 (283 KVO) with its Burlingham Seagull 60 body in Nottingham in March 1962. *Brian Botley*

Above: **During the 1950s Duple continued to produce new body designs, and the Elizabethan, for underfloor-engined chassis, was introduced in 1953. The Britannia, based on the Elizabethan but with vertical pillars, followed in 1955. Creamline of Borden was a purchaser of AEC Reliances with Britannia bodywork, and VHO 500 was acquired new in April 1959. Barton subsequently bought this bus and numbered it 914; it is seen here in Nottingham in July 1965.** *Brian Botley*

Below: **In May 1959 Robin Hood of Nottingham took delivery of a Duple Donington-bodied AEC Reliance, registered 249 CNN. This later became Barton's No 934, and is seen here on tour in July 1967.** *Mark Hampson collection*

Above: **The Harrington Cavalier was an instant success and significant advance orders were taken on the strength of the drawings alone. As early as August 1959 firm contracts for 10 coaches each had been placed by Timpsons and Northern General, and there were smaller orders for four from East Yorkshire and three from South Wales Transport. However, although the orders were in, Cavalier production did not get under way immediately. Once started, though, production soon gathered pace and the AEC Reliance** was the most popular chassis; of the first 40 Cavaliers, only four were Leyland. Although the front panels differed from body to body depending on the type of destination display fitted, the Cavalier was usually instantly recognisable by its strong 'smiling' moulding across the front. This is Barton's No 936 (99 GAL), a Harrington Cavalier-bodied AEC Reliance new in 1960 and seen in London on a tour to the South Coast in July 1966. *Brian Botley*

Left: Yeates of Loughborough was a company synonymous with 'unusual'-looking vehicles, fitted with plenty of chrome and looking rather flash, and it offered its own very individual styles right through to the 1960s. Between June and August 1962 Barton took delivery of six Yeates dual-doorway-bodied AEC Reliances, Nos 945 to 950 (945 to 950 MRR). They all had manual gearboxes and were stalwarts of the high-frequency route 15 between Ilkeston and Old Sawley. The rear doors were removed quite early in their life with Barton, circa 1965. This is No 950 (950 MRR) at Ilkeston Market Place in June 1966. On the right is No 785 (XAL 785), one of two Northern Counties-bodied AEC Regent Vs new to Barton in 1957. *Brian Botley*

Above: The first production Bedford VAL was designated VAL14, powered by a 6.17-litre Leyland 0.400 diesel engine mounted vertically at the front, and driving a Clark five-speed synchromesh gearbox (licence-built by Turner). The wheels were relatively small, at 16 inches in diameter, the same size as used on the Bedford J2 and VAS. The VAL had power steering and a tight turning circle, and at £1,775 was around £1,000 cheaper than either a Leyland or an AEC 36-foot chassis; it was also more than a ton lighter, yielding as a consequence an average fuel consumption of around 15 miles per gallon. Barton was among the first customers for the Bedford VAL14 and took delivery of seven with Yeates dual-doorway bodywork between June and July 1963. This is No 964 (964 RVO), one of four with C50D bodywork; the other three had DP56D bodies. *Mark Hampson collection*

Below: There is no mistaking which way to enter and exit No 965 (965 RVO) in this August 1966 view! *Brian Botley*

Above: **This is Barton's No 986 (986 VRR), a Harrington Grenadier-bodied AEC Reliance new in 1964. The Grenadier was constructed to take advantage of a change in legislation that permitted construction to a maximum width of 8ft 2½in, and its official debut was at the October 1962 Earls Court Commercial Motor Show.** *Mark Hampson collection*

Centre: **No 1000 in the Barton fleet was this Duple Vega Major-bodied Bedford VAL14 (ANN 700B), which was new in October 1964. This view was taken in the early summer of 1965, and standing alongside is Trent's NRC 160, a Willowbrook dual-purpose-bodied Leyland PSUC1/2 new in 1959.** *Brian Botley*

Right: **During June and July 1966 Barton took delivery of 10 Bedford VAM 5s, Nos 1071 to 1080 (FVO 71D to 80D), with Plaxton Panorama 1 bodies. This is No 1076 (FVO 76D) in the early summer of 1967.** *Mark Hampson collection*

Above: **RTL 761 (KYY 731), a Metro-Cammell-bodied Leyland PD2/1, started its service life with London Transport in May 1950 at Clay Hall depot. By 1957 it was allocated to Walworth, and in October 1958 was overhauled at Aldenham and transferred to Chalk Farm depot. In June 1972 the bus was purchased by Barton and numbered 1084; this view dates from September 1972.** *Mark Hampson collection*

lowbridge buses were no longer required. By 1964 most of the batch were appearing on works services, and the first to be taken out of service, Nos 199 to 202, went in early 1967. No 199 was sold to Barton and became No 1087 in that fleet; it is seen here in September 1972, just before its withdrawal from service and sale to the USA. *Mark Hampson collection*

Right: **In April and June 1954 Nottingham Corporation took delivery of 10 Park Royal-bodied AEC Regent IIIs, Nos 199 to 208 (SAU 199 to 208). These lowbridge buses were required due to a low railway bridge on Wilford Lane. From 1958 Clifton Bridge was opened over the Trent, so services to Clifton were moved to this new bridge and the**

Berresfords Motors

Berresfords was founded in 1923 by James Matthew Berresford and his wife Emily, operating from premises in Randles Lane, Wetley Rocks, near Leek in Staffordshire. Operations commenced on 3 February 1923 with a service between Hanley and Leek, altered later that year to Leek, Cellarhead, Werrington and Hanley. The next year this service was shared with PMT and F. Procter.

The Longton to Leek service of E. F. Millward of Cobridge was acquired in March 1930. During 1936 new premises were purchased at Windy Arbour in Cheddleton, and two years later Berresfords was formed into a limited company. By 1944 the fleet numbered ten buses. The garage was heightened for the use of double-deck buses, and the first, ED 7445, bought for £60, arrived in that year.

By the end of 1954 the company was operating a fleet of 18 vehicles – six coaches, eight single-deckers and four double-deckers – on a variety of school and works contracts, as well as two main stage services. In 1960 Byrne Brothers of Leek was taken over, bringing premises near Leek town centre and adding six coaches and a furniture van to the fleet. In 1963 W. Tatton & Sons of Leek was acquired, and the fleet then

stood at 28 vehicles, plus the six at Byrnes. Most buses at this time were acquired second-hand, but occasionally new coaches were still purchased. Interesting second-hand purchases were three ex-Silver Star Leyland Atlanteans in 1967, and a large batch of ex-Stockport Leyland PD2/1s between 1968 and 1970.

In 1947 Accrington Corporation took delivery of seven all-Leyland PD2s, Nos 108 to 114 (HTF 821 to 827), and between November 1960 and February 1962 Berresfords purchased five of them, HTF 821 and HTF 823 to HTF 826. This view of HTF 826 was taken in March 1962; the bus remained on fleet strength until January 1966. In the background on the left is JP 6689, a Bellhouse-bodied Leyland PS1 that was new in 1948, and was acquired from Smith of Donnington Wood in January 1955. *Brian Botley*

Above: **Byrne Brothers of Leek started business in 1922, became a limited company in July 1949, and by 1959 had a fleet of five buses. Control of the company was acquired by Berresfords in April 1960, and this included six buses and a furniture van. One of the six buses acquired was SBU 809, a Plaxton-bodied Ford 570E new in 1959, which remained in the Byrne/ Berresford fleet until withdrawal in March 1975.** *Brian Botley*

The bus immediately behind is another ex-Salford vehicle, CRJ 364, an MCCW-bodied Daimler CVG6 new in 1950, which was acquired in November 1965. This bus was sold to Audenshaw Diesels for scrap in February 1968. *Brian Botley*

Right: **Berresfords purchased a number of all-Leyland PD1As from Salford Corporation, and seen here in March 1966 is CRJ 322, which was new to Salford in 1948. This bus was scrapped in September 1967.**

Right: **The TS3 engine was used in the Commer Avenger Marks II, III and IV PSV chassis, and also in a number of Integral models from John C. Beadle and Thomas Harrington Ltd from 1952 to 1963. Initially these were a sales success, as they were more reliable and economical than the then current diesel-engined variant of the Bedford SB. However, the noise produced by the TS3 was not acceptable to tour operators and the higher body mounting compared with the SB required extra work for coachbuilders, and made**

the Avenger more expensive than the Bedford. Valiant Direct Coaches Ltd of Ealing took delivery of a Commer-Beadle coach, 26 LHX, in late 1957, and it was purchased by Berresfords from Howells & Withers of Pontllanfraith in March 1965, remaining in service until March 1968. This view was taken in the summer of 1967. *Brian Botley*

Below: **The Victor VT21L was introduced by Albion Motors Ltd in early 1963, designed primarily to suit Duple bodywork, and the**

complete vehicle had a maximum gross vehicle weight of 9 tons. The chassis was 17ft 8in long, and the engine was a Leyland 0.370 diesel engine, the drive being taken through an Albion GB.241 five-speed gearbox that could incorporate an overdrive sixth speed. Berresfords took two new Albion VT21Ls and Byrne Brothers one. This is URF 827C in the summer of 1969; it had Duple Firefly bodywork and was new to Berresfords in April 1965. *Brian Botley*

Above: **This view of RKE 540, a Saro-bodied Leyland Tiger Cub, was taken in November 1966. The bus was new to Maidstone & District in 1953 and was acquired by Berresfords in June 1966, lasting in service until June 1968. The car in the background is a Ford Anglia.** *Brian Botley*

Below: **Silver Star created quite a stir in 1959 when it became the first independent operator to purchase a Leyland PDR1/1 – its No 35, TMW 853, was only the 13th Leyland Atlantean to be built. The company went on to purchase a further three, one of which had coach bodywork. Sadly, Silver Star was acquired by Wilts & Dorset in June 1963 and the Atlanteans passed to Bristol Omnibus, which operated them from its Weston-super-Mare depot until September 1964, when they were acquired by Super Coaches of Upminster. Between April and December 1967 Berresfords purchased VAM 944, XMW 706 and 1013 MW, and this is the latter vehicle in the summer of 1969; it remained in service until February 1978.** *Brian Botley*

Above: This is DJA 189, an all-Leyland PD2 that had been new to Stockport Corporation in 1950 and was purchased by Berresfords in March 1968. This view was taken in September 1970, and the bus remained on fleet strength until April 1974.

Below: Birch Brothers purchased six Park Royal dual-purpose-bodied Leyland PSU3/4Rs in 1963, and from new they were regular performers on the company's route 203M between Rushden, Northamptonshire, and London. One of this batch, 92 FXD, was purchased by Berresfords from United Counties in June 1975, and this view was taken in the winter of that year. Note that the original front panel was damaged in an accident, and the replacement was from Seddon. *Mark Hampson collection*

Above: **Between March and April 1963 Southdown took delivery of 25 Marshall-bodied Leyland PSU3/1Rs, and most of the batch lasted in service until the mid-1970s. Berresfords acquired three in February 1977, and seen freshly painted in the company's livery in April 1977 is 265 AUF.** *Mark Hampson collection*

these were a feature of all Wigan Corporation buses and allowed the natives to distinguish Corporation buses from those of Ribble at night. They were painted out in GMT days as they were no longer needed. The car on the extreme left is the wonderful, in my opinion, Ford Capri.

Below: **Over a period of eight months from late 1975 to the middle of the following year, Berresfords acquired from Greater Manchester Transport four ex-Wigan Leyland PD2A/47s, three of which had Massey bodywork and the fourth Northern Counties. This is KEK 742 in Leek heading for Hanley in January 1976. Note that the bus still retains the little green lights at either side of the destination box;**

Blue Bus Services (Tailby & George)

During the 1920s a service began between Burton and Derby passing through Newton Solney, Repton, Willington and Findern. Despite fierce competition from the already established Trent Motor Traction service, it gradually grew; the company eventually became Tailby & George in 1927, and the service became known as the Blue Bus Service. In 1930 the business moved its operations to premises on Repton Road, Willington. A second route between Derby and Burton through Etwall, Egginton and Stretton was established around this time, and on 9 October 1939 the business became Tailby & George Ltd. During the Second World War the company began operating lowheight double-deck buses, due to the 13ft 6in clearance of the railway bridge in Willington. Later, new premises were built on the opposite side of the original Repton Road depot, opening in June 1956.

Blue Bus Services was well known for operating four of the rare Daimler CD650s, each with a Willowbrook lowbridge body. They were registered PRA 387 and 388, new in 1952, and SRB 424 and 425, new in 1953, and their fleet numbers were DR13 to DR16 respectively. The CD650 had a Daimler 10.6-litre six-cylinder diesel engine and a Daimler pre-select gearbox. Seen here is PRA 387 at Derby bus station in the summer of 1962. I think the sign on the building behind is excellent: 'The Gateway to Health – Co-op Milk'. *Brian Botley*

Above: **The second of the 1952 Daimler CD650s, with their impressive radiators, was PRA 388, seen here at the Willington depot in September 1966.**

Below: **Blue Bus Services buses were always maintained to the highest standard and, as** well as a steady programme of new buses, older buses were still available for service well into the early 1970s. This is YRB 483, a Willowbrook lowheight-bodied Daimler CVG6 that was new in 1955, and still performing service duties when this view was taken in April 1973. *Mark Hampson collection*

Right: **Dennis made an agreement with Bristol to build the Lodekka under licence as the Loline. This chassis was available with Gardner 6LW or 6LX, AEC AV470 or Leyland 0.600 engines. The Gardner 6LX engine, introduced in 1958, was a more powerful (10.45-litre) option to the 6LW and was soon the standard choice for most operators. A total of 48 Dennis Loline Is were built, the majority – 34 – going to Aldershot & District. Blue Bus Services purchased two of them, 465 FRB in 1957 and 303 GRB in 1958, both with Willowbrook bodywork, and the latter is seen here at Willington in February 1967.**

Centre: **Two Northern Counties-bodied Daimler CRG6LXs were purchased by Blue Bus Services in 1962, 325 YNU and, nearest the camera in this November 1963 view, 324 YNU. To the left is Trent's No 620 (620 CCH), a Northern Counties-bodied Daimler CRG6LX new in 1963. The bus on the right is NCB-bodied AEC Regent III KWB 86, new to Sheffield in 1947 and purchased by Stevenson's of Spath in March 1961.** *Brian Botley*

Right: **This is an example of the meticulous care that Blue Bus took in maintaining its fleet. Receiving a wash is No 26 (ARA 762B), a Northern Counties-bodied Daimler CRG6LX new in 1964.** *Mark Hampson collection*

Above: **This Duple Vega Major-bodied Bedford VAL14, KRB 426D, was purchased new in 1966 and is shown here shortly after the take-over of Blue Bus Services by Derby Corporation in 1974. The take-over cost Derby Corporation £212,039, for which it gained the depot at Willington and a fleet of 25 vehicles.** *Mark Hampson collection*

Below: **Also purchased in 1966 was No 27 (JRB 481D), a Northern Counties-bodied Daimler CRG6LX seen in Burton working the service via Repton to Derby in April 1967.** *Brian Botley*

Above: The Bedford VAL70 first appeared in December 1967 and was fitted with a Bedford 7.64-litre engine; at that time the total cost was around £7,500, of which £1,910 was for the chassis. Production of the VAL ceased in 1973, by which time a creditable 2,000 or more had been built. No other manufacturer has since produced a twin-steer PSV design. This view of Blue Bus Services' No 35 (YRB 203G), a Willowbrook-bodied Bedford VAL70, was taken in June 1970. *Brian Botley*

Below: The last new double-deck bus to be purchased by Blue Bus Services was No 28 (NRA 49J), an Alexander-bodied Daimler CRG6LX new in 1971. This view of the packed bus was taken in February 1972. *Mark Hampson collection*

Right: **In November 1948 Maidstone & District's No DH262 (KKK 868), a Weymann-bodied Bristol K6A, entered service and remained so until mid-1961. By October of that year it had been purchased by Fleet Car Sales of Dymchurch, and a month later was purchased by Charlton-on-Otmoor Services and entered service straight away. This view of KKK 868 was taken at the parking area for buses at Gloucester Green, Oxford, in April 1962. It remained in the fleet until its withdrawal in September 1963.** *Brian Botley*

Below right: **The Leyland TD5 became available in 1937 and had a 24-volt electrical system and an oil engine as standard. In early 1940 some late TD5s were frozen in production by Government order, but in late 1941 the stocks were unfrozen and finished so that the Titan line could be closed, enabling space for tank production. In 1939 Maidstone & District took delivery of a Leyland Titan TD5 (FKO 223), which operated for Chatham & District as No 293 from new until 1942, when it returned to M&D. After its withdrawal the bus was purchased by Charlton-on-Otmoor Services and was photographed standing beside KKK 868 at Gloucester Green, also in April 1962.** *Brian Botley*

Above: On 10 June 1938 EUF 192, a Beadle-bodied Leyland TD5, entered service with Southdown Motor Services. It remained with Southdown until late February 1956, and was then purchased by Hutfield Coaches (Gosport) on 1 March, and had a rear door added. The bus then passed to Hutfield Coaches (Warwick) Ltd in June 1956, and later to Charlton-on-Otmoor Services; it is seen here at Gloucester Green in February 1962. The bus on the right is City of Oxford No 189 (189 AWL), a Weymann-bodied AEC Regent V new in 1956. To the left is 332 BHA, one of a pair of Leyland PSUC1/2s with Duple centre-doorway coach bodywork that were new to Gilderways of Smethwick in May 1956. This bus was acquired by Charlton-on-Otmoor Services in September 1962. *Brian Botley*

Below: In December 1965 a Harrington-bodied Leyland PSUC1/2 coach, 416 DHA, was purchased from Gilderways of Smethwick by Charlton-on-Otmoor Services. Together with three similar coaches, it had been new to Gilderways in May 1957, and is seen here in May 1966. *Brian Botley*

Right: **Timpsons Coaches took delivery of this coach, TGJ 488, a Beadle-Commer Integral, in 1956. By the time this view was taken in April 1963 at Gloucester Green, Oxford, it had passed to Charlton-on-Otmoor Services.** *Brian Botley*

Centre: **In July 1949 RT 1525 (KGU 239), a Park Royal-bodied AEC Regent, entered service with London Transport at Middle Row depot in Kensington. On overhaul in Aldenham in July 1965 it was fitted with a Saunders roofbox body and was allocated to Upton depot until March 1968. After storage it was purchased by Charlton-on-Otmoor Services in December 1968 and was a regular performer for the business until withdrawal in December 1975. This view was taken at Gloucester Green in August 1972. The car on the extreme left is, I think, a Triumph Vitesse.** *Brian Botley*

Right: **Standing at Gloucester Green in August 1971 is Charlton-on-Otmoor's EAY 700C, a Plaxton-bodied AEC Reliance that was new to N&S Coaches of Oadby near Leicester in May 1965.** *Brian Botley*

Right: **Rhondda Transport took delivery of 20 Metro-Cammell-bodied AEC Regents Vs in 1961, and by the time this view was taken in September 1976 one of the batch, 456 KTG, had been acquired by Charlton-on-Otmoor Services. The company's depot was always well worth a visit if you happened to be passing that way. For many years the fleet contained predominantly AEC-built buses and coaches, some of which were second-hand double-deckers. The use of colour-coordinated destination blinds was a nice touch. There was always a Charlton Services bus outstationed during school term-time behind the Shotover Arms at Risinghurst, so that it could do the school run from Risinghurst to Wheatley Upper and Lower Schools, and it was often an AEC Regent.** *Mark Hampson collection*

Below: **To supplement the Cavalier for the 1963 season, the Grenadier was introduced; it was outwardly similar to the Cavalier but the glazing was revised, employing one fewer window per side and dipping less** toward the rear. A larger windscreen was also fitted, with a more prominent peak, and only the rear glass was carried over from the Cavalier. Revised front and rear mouldings were employed, and forced ventilation was standard. Barton's Nos 979 to 988 (979 to 988 VRR), AEC Reliances, had Cavalier-type windscreens and roof-mounted destination boxes, as well as air operation for the coach door, enabling use as a bus. This is 988 VRR in the fleet of Charlton Services in April 1975. *Mark Hampson collection*

Chiltern Queens

Right: **One of Chiltern Queens' first purchases were three Duple bus-bodied AEC Reliances, LMO 743 to 745, which were delivered in 1955. This view of LMO 745 was taken at Reading General railway station in July 1969. The bus in the background is a Thames Valley ECW-bodied Bristol FLF.** *Brian Botley*

Below right: **New in October 1952 to Yellow Bus Services, SPD 207 was a Dennis L6 Falcon with Gurney Nutting B30F bodywork. Yellow Bus Services was taken over by Aldershot & District in June 1958 and the bus was acquired later by Chiltern Queens and is seen here in Reading in April 1960. Coachbuilder J. Gurney Nutting & Co Ltd was founded in 1918 as a new enterprise by a Croydon firm of builders and joiners of the same name; it specialised in sporting bodies, and built the body for Malcolm Campbell's 1931** *Bluebird* **world speed record car. With the outbreak of the Second World War all coachbuilding work was suspended, and during the war Gurney Nutting built boats, from lifeboats to patrol boats. In**

1945 the business was renamed Gurney Nutting Ltd, styling itself as 'coachbuilders and engineers', and became part of the Jack Barclay group. It also built full-size bus and coach bodies, and was still producing these in late 1952, closing some time afterwards. *Brian Botley*

Right: **The Dennis Pelican, with Duple Midland bodywork, was produced in 1956 as a demonstrator and registered 530 BPG; after little interest, it was sold to Yellow Bus Services of Stoughton, Guildford. That company was acquired by Aldershot & District in 1958, and the bus passed to Trimdon Bus Service, County Durham. Trimdon then sold it to Daisy Bus Service of Brigg, Lincolnshire, and in 1962 the bus eventually arrived at Chiltern Queens. In 1970 the chassis was scrapped and the body, after frontal modifications, was fitted to an AEC Reliance, YNX 478, which is seen here at Reading station in September 1972.** *Mark Hampson collection*

Below right: **At Chiltern Queens' depot in August 1968 is KBV 778, a Plaxton Consort-bodied AEC Reliance that was new to Batty Holt Ribblesdale of Blackburn in 1958. The Consort was first shown at the 1956 Commercial Motor Show and was a development of the Venturer, but in place of the previous oval the four-part grille was now enclosed by a near hexagonal outline, wider at the top than the bottom, with the headlamps outside. Trim was revised to be much squarer in outline, featuring ribbed brightwork, and the curved rear quarter lights, first standardised on the Venturer III, were now incorporated into the main window line. However, a year later the Consort II was announced, re-introducing the oval grille outline of the Venturer,** but now surrounding a plainer grille with chrome flash across the middle, while the trim lines, so recently squared up, were softened once again. The evident popularity of the oval-shaped grille ensured its survival as a Plaxton hallmark for many years to come. The Consort III and IV had a new silver-effect dished oval grille with a chrome flash through the middle, and a curved windscreen with a central division. For the 1961 coaching season the Consort IV evolved into the Embassy, the main change being that the windows now tapered inwards towards the roof rather than being vertical. Chiltern Queens' fleet had two liveries, red and cream for the buses and green and turquoise for the coaches, which I think looked very smart.

Right: **Wallace Arnold was one of the UK's largest holiday coach tour operators, founded in 1912 and named after its founders, Wallace Cunningham and Arnold Crowe. During 1955 Wallace Arnold took delivery of a large batch of Burlingham-bodied AEC Reliances, one of which was UUG 39. This coach later passed to Chiltern Queens and is seen at the company's depot in August 1968.**

Centre and below right: **Aldershot & District took delivery of 15 Park Royal coach-bodied AEC Reliances in 1963, and they were regular performers on services to Victoria Coach Station. This is 474 FCG from that batch, and the first view shows it fitted with bus seats and in the fleet of Chiltern Queens at Reading railway station in November 1976. This bus later passed to Panther Bus of Crawley and regularly worked on that company's 107 service between Horsham and Brighton. The second view was taken in the same place in May 1976. Unfortunately the bus was destroyed by fire in March 1991.** *Mark Hampson collection/ author*

Right: **During 1957 Aldershot & District took delivery of 30 Weymann dual-purpose-bodied AEC Reliances, Nos 283 to 312 (RCG 601 to 630). Between 1968 and 1970 all were withdrawn by Aldershot & District, and one, RCG 618, found its way into the fleet of Chiltern Queens, and is seen here in Reading in June 1971.** *Brian Botley*

Centre: **WVA 453, seen here in Reading in March 1972, was one of a pair of AEC Reliances with Willowbrook B45F bodywork that had been new to Irvine, Golden Eagle Coaches, of Salsburgh, near Motherwell, in May 1960, and were acquired by OK Motor Services in March 1965. After withdrawal in December 1971, WVA 453 passed to Chiltern Queens, which operated it until May 1977 and scrapped it in 1981. The other bus, WVA 454, was withdrawn by OK nine months earlier and spent the rest of its life in North Yorkshire, initially with Primrose Valley of Filey.** *Mark Hampson collection*

Right: **Shipley of Ashton-under-Lyne purchased two Yeates coach-bodied AEC Reliances in 1960, registered 25 and 26 MTF. This view of the latter was taken in August 1968, by which time the coach was part of the Chiltern Queens**

W. Gash & Sons (Newark)

fleet. *Brian Botley*

Right: **This is No B8 (GAL 966), a Bedford OWB that originally had Duple utility bodywork and was new to W. Gash & Sons Ltd in 1944. It was rebodied with a standard OB body by Duple in May 1952. This view was taken in September 1963 at the Bowbridge Road depot in Newark. No B8 was withdrawn from service in September 1964, and passed to Langston & Tasker of Steeple Claydon, Buckinghamshire.** *Brian Botley*

Below right: **From the start of passenger carrying in 1922, services gradually expanded, including a through service to Nottingham, while the development of aerodromes at Syerston and Newton brought increased traffic during the Second World War. The post-war years saw the first of the company's Daimler CVD6 double-deckers arrive in 1948. This is No DD2 (KAL 579), which was new in November 1948 and originally had a Strachan lowbridge** body. **It was rebodied by Massey in 1958 and was in the Gash fleet until its withdrawal in August 1979, and is now in preservation. It is seen here at Bowbridge Road depot in August 1974.** *Mark Hampson collection*

Above: **This is W. Gash & Sons' No DD3 (KAL 580), a Daimler CVD6 new in November 1948 and rebodied by Massey in 1958, on the Newark to Nottingham service in April 1975. No DD3 was withdrawn from service in August 1979. The yellow car on the left is an instantly recognisable Ford Escort.** *Mark Hampson collection*

Below: **Standing at Bowbridge Road depot in June 1969 is No DD6 (KNN 959), a Roberts-bodied Daimler CVD6 new to Gash in August 1949. Nos DD5 and DD6 were the first highbridge double-deckers in the Gash fleet, following the lowering of the road beneath the Saxondale railway bridge on the A46. No DD6 received platform doors in 1957 and was withdrawn from service in December 1978.** *Brian Botley*

Right: **This is Gash's No DD9 (MRR 8), a Duple-bodied Daimler CVD6 purchased new in 1951, although it had originally been intended for the Oxfordshire-based operator Smith of Upper Heyford. This view was taken at the Bowbridge Road depot in September 1964. After withdrawal in 1978, No DD9 was sadly converted into a 'tree-lopper' by the company, having part of its upper saloon removed in the process, and was sold for scrap in 1979.** *Brian Botley*

Below: **Daimler offered a purpose-built own-make engine for the Freeline; it was called the D650H and was derived from the D650 engine used in the rare post-war CD650 double-decker. The swept volume was 10.6 litres, and the major difference from the vertical version was the sump casting. Commonality of parts was such that CD650 operators could, and did, use the 'top end' of the horizontal engine when they could not get spares for the vertical version. Output was originally 125bhp at 1,650rpm, but this was soon raised to 150bhp at 2,000rpm, which was class-leading power in 1953, and the model code for this version was D650HS. Gash took delivery of the first two production Daimler Freeline D650HSs in 1952; they were registered NAL 782 and 783 and bodied by Burlingham. This view was taken at the back of Bowbridge Road depot in June 1962. Both coaches were sold to Trent Concrete in 1967 for use as staff buses.** *Brian Botley*

Above: **No DD10 (RAL 795) was a Massey-bodied Daimler CVG6 new to Gash in 1954, and was the only tin-fronted double-decker in the fleet. This picture was taken in Newark in September 1971; the bus was finally withdrawn from passenger service in the mid-1980s.** *Mark Hampson collection*

Below: **W. Gash & Sons of Newark was noted for it bus operations, and in particular its elderly Daimler double-deckers, which had been bought new, but the company also had a modern coach fleet painted in an attractive off-white with light turquoise and dark blue relief. This is No B24 (KNN 699E), a Plaxton Panorama-bodied Bedford VAS1 bought new in 1967, leaving the Bowbridge Road depot for a schools service in August 1972. This coach was later bought from DSB Coach Sales near Loughborough by Brutonian for a school contract into Bishop's Caundle School in Dorset, and spent a few months in that company's fleet in 1986/87 before being written off by a nearly new car on a school run.** *Mark Hampson collection*

Looking very lonely and forgotten in this August 1973 view is No B25 (NVO 698F), a Plaxton-bodied Bedford VAS5 new to Gash in 1968. *Mark Hampson collection*

Green Bus Company

In 1927, C. J. Whieldon, who had previously been a driver with Stevenson's of Spath, started a business on his own. In April 1930 premises at 56 Bridge Street, Uttoxeter, were acquired, and in the same year the trading name of Green Bus was in use. Services commenced from Uttoxeter to Lichfield, and to Hednesford, which was later extended to Cannock via Rugeley. Two garages and a large area of land were purchased at Westbrook in Rugeley, and a limited company was formed in January 1958.

In 1946 Foden launched the PVSC6, which had a Gardner 6LW 8.4-litre six-cylinder diesel engine with the option of a Gardner 5LW 7.0-litre, the PVSC5. In 1949 the Foden FE6 4-litre two-stroke PVFE6 diesel engine became available, but only 52 were made. Green Bus Company No 40 (URF 873) was a Foden PVFE6 with a rare King & Taylor FB38F body, new in 1951. In 1964 it was fitted with an FD6 engine but was withdrawn in September 1967, becoming a towing vehicle until scrapped in 1968. This view was taken in February 1967. *Brian Botley*

Above: **Green Bus purchased two Burlingham Seagull Guy Arab LUF 6HLW coaches in May 1958, numbered 3 and 11 (499 and 500 URF). This view of No 3 was taken in September 1969; by April of the following year the bus had been withdrawn from service.** *Brian Botley*

1963. Green Bus purchased five of them, JOW 917 to 920 and JOW 922, between March and April 1965, by which time all had been rebuilt to forward entrance. This is No 23 (JOW 922) in August 1968. *Brian Botley*

Right: **In 1952 and 1955 Southampton Corporation took delivery 12 Park Royal-bodied Guy Arab LUF 6HLWs, JOW 917 to 928, which were all originally fitted with dual doors. Twelve of the chassis were new in 1952 but only six were bodied in that year, the remainder in 1955. The first six were originally destined to provide a new type of service, giving more standing room over seat places. Loading was to be through a rear door with passengers purchasing tickets from a seated conductor. The first six were reseated from 26 to 36 in 1955, but only lasted in service until**

Above: **Nearest the camera is all-Leyland PD2/3 No 32 (DRN 258), which was new to Ribble in 1950 and purchased by Green Bus in May 1965. Behind is No 34 (BSD 287), an NCME-bodied Daimler CVG6 that had been new to Western SMT in 1952 and was acquired in July 1965. The Daimler lasted a little over two years in the Green Bus fleet, whereas the Leyland was not withdrawn until May 1969.** *Brian Botley*

Below: **On 14 September 1969 the last two routes of Birch Brothers, 203 and 203M, were passed to United Counties together with 12** vehicles, and the company's Rushden garage was sold. The bus operations of Birch Brothers were no more, although the coaches ran for a couple more years from Kentish Town. On 1 February 1971 the business and the coaches were sold to the George Ewer Group, and the Birch name faded from the public transport scene for ever. Between late 1960 and early 1961 Birch Brothers had purchased five Willowbrook AEC Reliance coaches, 44 to 48 AUW, and during May and June 1970 Green Bus purchased four of them, becoming Nos 16 to 19. This is No 19 (48 AUW), photographed a few months after purchase. *Brian Botley*

Right: **Stratford Blue Motors purchased three Willowbrook-bodied Leyland PD2/12s in 1956, but they had a relatively short service life with that fleet. Two of the batch, TNX 455 and 456, were acquired by Green Bus in November 1967, and this view of No 30 (TNX 455) was taken in July 1971.** *Brian Botley*

Below: **In March 1969 the first Seddon Pennine RU was built; registered TBU 598G, it was used as a demonstrator, visiting many operators. In May 1971 Green Bus purchased the vehicle and gave it the fleet number 23. This view was taken a short time before Green Bus was absorbed by Midland Red in 1973. Very few of the company's buses saw service beyond the take-over, and** certainly the older buses would never turn a wheel with their new owners, but were quickly despatched to the breaker's yard. *Brian Botley*

Harper Brothers (Heath Hayes)

Mr C. G. Harper commenced a service between Heath Hayes and Cannock in the early 1920s. By the 1930s the main stage service had been extended from Heath Hayes through Brownhills to Aldridge, and during the war the service reached Kingstanding to link with Birmingham City Transport. Two businesses were acquired during the war, Homer of Cannock and Reynolds of Cannock. In 1946 Johnson of Aldridge was acquired, followed in the 1950s by Sanders of Chasetown and Dunn & Hale Ltd of Brownhills. In June 1960 the business of Hastilow & Son of Sutton Coldfield was purchased.

By 1965 the main stage carriage services of the company were Cannock to Birmingham and Lichfield to Kingstanding, working from depots at Heath Hayes, Cannock and Aldridge. On 22 April 1974 the business of Harper Brothers (Heath Hayes) Ltd and its wholly owned subsidiary Tudor Rose Coaches of Sutton Coldfield were acquired by Midland Red, involving the transfer of the company's garage at Hednesford Road, 50 vehicles, and 89 full-time staff; control formerly passed to Midland Red on 7 September 1974.

Above and top right: **A licence was held by Harper Brothers for seasonal journeys to Butlins at Pwllheli. On this seasonal service in July 1959 is No 28 (1031 E), a Burlingham Seagull-bodied Leyland PSU1/11 that was new to the company in May 1953. By comparison, the second view shows the same bus after having been fitted with a flat front and converted to dual-purpose in February 1968.** *Both Brian Botley*

Above: In July 1959 a further two Burlingham Seagull-bodied coaches were purchased new, this time on Guy Arab LUF chassis. They were numbered 59 and 60, and seen in October 1968 is No 60 (1294 RE). Alongside is an ex-St Helens Park Royal-bodied AEC Regent III new in1951, which was purchased by Harper's in April 1962. No 60 is now in preservation. *Brian Botley*

Above: **St Helens Corporation took delivery of 25 Park Royal-bodied AEC Regent IIIs during 1951; numbered 1-25 (BDJ 801 to 825), they had a relatively short service life in that fleet, the last being withdrawn in 1962. Between November 1961 and April 1964 Harper Brothers built up a small fleet of them when a total of seven were purchased. This is No 15 (BDJ 806), purchased in July 1962 and seen here in the late summer of 1964. The** cars in the background are, from left to right, a Standard, a Ford and a new 1100. *Mark Hampson collection*

Below: **This is Cannock bus station in September 1968, and the bus is No 9 (BDJ 807), which was the last of the ex-St Helens AEC Regent IIIs purchased by Harper's, arriving in April 1964.** *Brian Botley*

Above: **No 27 (HBF 679D)** was one of a pair (with HBF 680D) of Leyland PD2A/27s with MCCW bodywork delivered new to Harper Brothers at Heath Hayes in 1966; it is seen here in September 1968. Both buses passed to Midland Red on the take-over of Harper's, and a little later in No 27's life it received a coat of all-over yellow paint and started a new role as a Midland Red driver trainer. It eventually became the driver trainer at Leicester. Passing to a group of Midland Fox drivers for preservation, a start was made on restoring it to original condition. It was donated to Wythall in late 1997, and repainted back into Harper Brothers livery in 2003. *Brian Botley*

Right: **No 11 (888 DUK)** was a Strachan-bodied Guy Arab V, new in 1963; originally a demonstrator, it was bought by Harper Brothers in May 1966. It was originally in an unpainted white livery, with two green stripes and a green bonnet, which earned it the nickname among Harpers' staff of 'the old grey mare'. This view of No 11 in Harper Brothers livery dates from the summer of 1973. *Brian Botley*

Above: **The last half-cab purchased new by Harper's was No 23 (NRF 349F), an NCME-bodied Leyland PD3A/5 that was delivered during May 1968. This view was taken in February 1974, just a few weeks ahead of the take-over by Midland Red.** *Mark Hampson collection*

Below: **Following the purchase of the last new half-cab bus in May 1968, Harper Brothers turned to Daimler for its next new double-deck** buses. **Two NCME-bodied Daimler CRG6LXs were delivered in May 1970, and in July 1971 two further examples, also with NCME bodywork, were purchased. One of them was No 31 (BRE 311J), seen at Cannock in March 1972. This bus passed to Midland Red on 7 September 1974 and was almost immediately fitted for one-person operation. It was withdrawn by Midland Red North in February 1984.** *Mark Hampson collection*

House's (Watlington)

Above: **At House's depot at Watlington in September 1967 we see DUD 810, a Bedford OB with Duple Vista bodywork bought new in 1948. The bus in the garage is WXC 347, a Bedford SB, which was purchased second-hand by the company.**

Below: **This is Marine Parade in Brighton in the glorious sunshine of March 1966, and in view is House's UVN 490), a Plaxton-bodied Ford 570E that I think had been new to Brown of Helperby in 1959.** *Brian Botley*

Standing at the depot of House's of Watlington in the winter of 1964 is OFC 489, a Commer Avenger purchased new by the company in 1950. *Brian Botley*

Hulley's (Baslow)

The BMMO S9 single-deck bus had 40-seat Brush bodywork and an underfloor engine, and 100 entered service with Midland Red during 1949. Hulley's purchased two S9s, LHA 358 in January 1963 and LHA 400 in May of that year, and this is the latter, seen on a very wet day in May 1964. The original 40 seats were increased to 44 by Roe during 1952. This bus was withdrawn from service in August 1968 and sold for scrap in February the following year. *Brian Botley*

This is TWP 967, a petrol-engined Bedford SB3 with 41-seat Duple Vega coachwork, which had been bought new in December 1957 by Eric Harrison at Broadway, a close relative of Edmund Harrison, who ran Broadway Coaches. Consequent upon his death, Eric Harrison's two-coach business was taken over by Broadway Coaches in October 1958, with TWP 967 being operated until May 1960, when it was sold to David Crockett's Golden Valley Motors at Hereford. After a short time with E. Thorpe & Co of Thurgoland, in September 1961 the bus was acquired by Hulley's of Baslow and fitted with a Bedford 330 diesel engine in July 1970; it remained in the fleet until June 1976, and is seen in the first view in March 1971. The second photograph is dated August 1969. *Brian Botley/Mark Hampson collection*

Above: **The last Bedford OB acquired by Hulley's was JNN 174, which had Duple bodywork and had been new to Barton in December 1947. It was fitted with a Perkins P6 diesel engine in 1951 and remained with Barton until April 1957, when it was acquired by Thomas of North Muskham. Hulley's purchased the bus in March 1960 and it remained in the fleet until September 1969, when it was scrapped. It is seen here in the winter of 1968.**

Below: **This is EBV 850, a Yeates-bodied Bedford SBG that had been new to Barry Holt of Blackburn in September 1953. B. & H. Goldfine of Salford acquired the bus in October 1956 and it reached the fleet of Hulley's in May 1962. This view was taken in August 1968, just a few months before the bus was withdrawn from service in February of the following year and sold for scrap.**

Above: **Between August 1959 and March 1962, Sheffield Corporation, Sheffield Joint Transport Committee and the Sheffield Railways fleets took delivery of 36 Leyland L1s. The bodywork chosen for them included examples by Weymann, Burlingham and ECW. In January 1960 five Weymann coach-bodied L1s were delivered, registered 6170 to 6174 WJ, and Hulley's purchased all five in August 1971; 6173 WJ is seen here in December of that year. One of the batch, 6172 WJ, was not operated by Hulley's, but was used as a source of spares, and 6174 WJ was the last to be withdrawn, in April 1978. All five passed** to Ensign of Grays in August 1978 and were scrapped in Carlton. *Brian Botley*

Below: **In September 1962 R. Armstrong of Ebchester purchased new Yeates Pegasus bus-bodied Bedford SB5 2626 UP. It was subsequently bought by Raisbeck of Bedlington in August 1967, then in July 1970 was acquired by C. Bartle of Outwood. Hulley's purchased the bus in April 1972, and this view was taken a few months later. 2626 UP was withdrawn in August 1978 and purchased for preservation, but unfortunately was sold for scrap in early 1980.** *Mark Hampson collection*

Right: **The Perkins R6 engine was developed too quickly and not properly tested, and left many customers dissatisfied. The Bedford SBO was fitted with it, and one of the customers for this bus was Southern Vectis, which purchased 11 with Duple bodywork between 1955 and 1957. This is ODL 48, one of that batch, new to Southern Vectis in February 1957, and seen here in May 1976. The bus passed to United Counties in December 1967, entering service in May 1968 having been fitted with a Perkins P6 diesel engine. A few months later Twell of Ingham purchased the vehicle, and it passed to the fleet of Smaller of Barton-on-Humber before being returning to Twell in October 1969. Hulley's then purchased it for spares, but it entered service** in August 1973. The car behind is a Renault 5, which was first introduced to the public on 10 December 1971. The early production version used a dashboard-mounted gearshift, later replaced with a floor-mounted shifter. Door handles were formed by a cut-out in the door panel and pillar. It was one of the first cars produced with plastic (polyester and glass fibre) bumpers, which have since become an industry standard. *Mark Hampson collection*

Below: **Some miners' organisations and the National Coal Board itself sometimes provided their own transport for miners, and Maltby Miners' Welfare purchased this new Duple Midland-bodied Bedford SBO,** PET 100, in January 1957. It passed to J. O. Andrew of Sheffield in August 1969, then to Wigmore's of Dinnington later that year, and was purchased by Hulley's in August 1971. This photograph was taken in February 1972, and the bus remained with Hulley's, then Silver Service, until it was retired after a service life of 22 years in October 1979, being purchased for preservation in February 1980. Maltby coal mine was until recently one of only five remaining deep mines in the UK, the others being Daw Mill in the West Midlands (which closed during 2013), Harworth in Nottinghamshire, Kellingley in Yorkshire and Thoresby in Nottinghamshire. *Mark Hampson collection*

Above: In May 1958 J. Freeman of Blackpool purchased a Bedford SB3 (NFV 296), which was fitted with a diesel engine and had Duple Vega coachwork. By November 1960 the bus was with Gould of Rotherham, and in July 1961 was acquired by Furness of High Green. It reached Hulley's in August 1967 from Kerrigan, Conisbrough, and remained in the fleet until 1975. To the left of the coach in this view taken in February 1972 is BMMO C5 795 GHA, which had been purchased by Hulley's in May 1971. Main production of the C5 began in 1958, and by the following autumn the first 24 had entered service. These production buses featured the 'Dutch lantern'-style windscreens and had four-speed manual gearboxes and the normally aspirated BMMO 8.028-litre diesel engine. They were later upgraded to a five-speed overdrive gearbox. By the end of 1971 all but one of the C5s and its variations had been withdrawn. On the extreme left is ex-Yorkshire Traction No 922 (DHE 353), a Brush-bodied Leyland PSU1/9 new in May 1951 and acquired by Hulley's in May 1965. This bus was withdrawn from service in June 1968 and was repainted and refurbished in September 1971, but was very rarely used. *Brian Botley*

Below: This view of NPM 315F, a Ford R226 with Strachan coachwork, was taken in August 1975. It had been new to Woburn Garages, trading as Evan Evans, of London WC1 in March 1968, and subsequently passed into the ownership of Wallace Arnold in February 1969. It reached Hulley's in November 1974, after service with Greenhalgh & Pennington of Longton, and entered service in July 1975. Webster's of Hognaston had the bus for a few months in late 1979, but it returned to Hulley's in December 1979 as a source of spares, and had been scrapped by March 1983. *Brian Botley*

In August 1978 Silver Service purchased five ECW-bodied Bristol FLF6Gs from Western SMT; they were registered VCS 366 to 368, VCS 370 and VCS 375. All except VCS 368 entered service with Hulley's; the last to do so, in March 1979, was VCS 367, seen here in November 1979. This bus was withdrawn in May 1980 and later exported to Zambia. The bus whose rear end can be seen on the left is FKF 901F, an MCW-bodied Leyland PSUR1A/1R new to Liverpool Corporation in 1968. It was purchased in May 1979, and by April 1980 a total of seven Leyland PSUR1A/1Rs had been acquired from Merseyside Passenger Transport Executive.

Hylton & Dawson (Glenfield)

Hylton & Dawson was one of the last traditional independent operators running a stage service into the city of Leicester. The company's route from the village of Glenfield through Leicester's north-western suburbs had its origins in 1923, when the company started business.

Standing at Leicester bus station in July 1967 is RPG 807, an all-Leyland PSU1 Royal Tiger. Eight models were offered for the domestic market, designated PSU1/9 to PSU1/16, all with a 15ft 7in wheelbase and an overall width of either 7ft 6in (PSU1/9-12) or 8 feet (PSU1/13-16).

F. Procter & Sons (Hanley)

The business of F. Procter was started in 1922, and by 1923 was licensed to operate on the Hanley to Leek service worked jointly with Berresford Motors and Potteries Motor Traction.

Right: **Working route 16 between Hanley and Leek in August 1967 is ex-London Transport RT 4420 (NXP 774). This bus was purchased in June 1963 and lasted in the service fleet until May 1969.** *Brian Botley*

Below: **Leaving Hanley bus station in May 1970 for the journey to Leek is 4559 VC, a Northern Counties-bodied Daimler CRG6, which began life as a Daimler** demonstrator in 1962. **The bus was purchased by Procter's in August 1964.**

Above: **In February 1965 Procter's purchased new Daimler CRG6 AVT 249C with Alexander bodywork. This view was taken at Hanley bus station in November 1969.** *Brian Botley*

Below: **Also leaving Hanley bus station in May 1970 is PEH 238F, an Alexander-bodied Daimler CRG6, new to Procter's in January 1968.**

Red Rover (Aylesbury)

Right: **London Transport RT 212 (HLW 199), an AEC Regent III with a Park Royal roofbox body, entered service in November 1947 from Potters Bar depot. During 1957 it was transferred to Norwood and was then stored until November 1958. In that month the bus was sold to Bird's of Stratford-upon-Avon and very quickly purchased by Red Rover. This view of HLW 199 was taken in Aylesbury in October 1965, and a little over two years later the bus was sold to North's in Leeds and scrapped.** *Brian Botley*

Below: **This is KGU 434, the former RTL 358, a Park Royal-bodied Leyland PD2/1 that was new to London Transport in September 1949 and began its service life from Hammersmith depot. In January 1957 the bus was transferred to Barking and three months later was overhauled at Aldenham Works. From there it was transferred to Seven** Kings depot, where it worked until November 1958, and in that month was purchased by **Red Rover of Aylesbury. This is the Bicester Road depot of Red Rover in October 1968.** *Brian Botley*

Above: **This is ROD 765, a Metro-Cammell-bodied AEC Regent V new to Devon General in 1956, one of many bought by that company fitted with platform doors for rural services. This bus was withdrawn by Devon General in 1968 and purchased by Red Rover. It is seen here in August 1975, and remained in the Red Rover fleet until late 1977; it has since passed into preservation.** *Mark Hampson collection*

Right: **Standing in the Bicester Road depot on a miserable day in October 1968 is 6116 BH, an AEC Bridgemaster with Park Royal bodywork that was a cancelled order for Baxter's of Airdrie and was new in February 1963. It passed to the fleet of Bicester Coaches in late 1976.** *Brian Botley*

Above: AEC Bridgemasters were not sold in great numbers other than to AEC-dominated fleets, or if there were low bridges in their area of operations. The Bicester route of Red Rover had a low bridge between Marsh Gibbon and Launton that AEC Bridgemasters could negotiate. This is 27 WKX, seen in August 1975, a Park Royal-bodied AEC Bridgemaster that was purchased new by Red Rover in April 1962. *Mark Hampson collection*

Right: The AEC Swift was a rear-engined single-deck bus chassis built between 1964 and 1974. The chassis design was closely related to the Leyland Panther and it was available in lengths of 33 and 36 feet, with

an AEC AH505 or AH691 engine. Red Rover purchased a Willowbrook-bodied AEC Swift in August 1967, and this photograph of XBH 55F was taken at the Bicester Road depot in October 1968. *Brian Botley*

Between February and June 1965 Nottingham Corporation took delivery of 35 Weymann-bodied AEC Regent Vs, DAU 351C to 385C. They were relatively short-lived in the Nottingham fleet and five were purchased by Red Rover. This is DAU 358C, just arrived from Nottingham in the summer of 1976. When Luton & District acquired Red Rover, this bus remained in the fleet as a driver trainer into the late 1980s.

On the left is EPH 189B, a Willowbrook-bodied AEC Reliance that had been new to Safeguard of Guildford in October 1964. Quite a number of operators, Red Rover among them, were grateful to Safeguard, which seemed to pursue quite an active vehicle replacement policy, for being able to supply them with good-quality late-model service buses when it had finished with them. *Mark Hampson collection*

Shropshire Independents

During 1958 Stringfellow of Wigan purchased DJP 20, a Yeates-bodied Bedford SB8, which had a Leyland O.350 engine fitted. In April 1962 this bus was purchased by R. A. Price of Excelsior Garage, Wrockwardine Wood, near Telford, and it is seen working the Shrewsbury to Wrockwardine Wood service in August 1964. *Brian Botley*

Right: **In 1964 Williamson's Motorways of Shrewsbury had a Wednesday-and-Saturday-only service from Barker Street in Shrewsbury to Oldwoods (Miller's Shop). Leaving Barker Street for Oldwoods in August 1964 is DEN 550, a Duple Vega-bodied Bedford SB.** *Brian Botley*

Centre: **Standing at Victoria Street in Wellington waiting to make a journey to Oakengates in July 1964 is EUX 183, a Burlingham bus-bodied Crossley SD42 that was new to G. Cooper & Sons in 1948. The Crossley SD42 range of single-deck buses was built between 1947 and 1952. For the home market, 111 of them were completed as buses and 625 as coaches; 191 of the latter had Crossley bodywork, the remainder being supplied to independent coachbuilders.** *Brian Botley*

Right: **A. T. Brown of Trench, Telford, was one of the operators of the Shropshire Omnibus Association and ran, in a rota, the daily service to Donnington from Victoria Street, Wellington. Standing in Victoria Street in August 1964 is VDA 32, a Willowbrook bus-bodied Guy Warrior that was new as a Guy demonstrator in 1958, and was purchased by Brown's in January 1959.** *Brian Botley*

Above: **In 1964 Valley Motors of Bishop's Castle ran a daily service between there and Shrewsbury, together with other market day services. Standing in Barker Street in Shrewsbury in August 1964 is SWP 554, a Duple-bodied Bedford SBG that was new in 1957, and which Valley Motors had purchased from M&M of Kidderminster in May 1963. The SBG had Bedford's own 4.927-litre petrol engine fitted as new. The magnificent car on the left with the visor is a Vauxhall Velox pre-1955-facelift model.** *Brian Botley*

Below: **A. J. Boulton commenced bus services just after the First World War. In 1953 the business of Central Garage, Church Stretton, was acquired, and in August 1959 A. E. Freeman of Munslow was taken over. Boulton's Bus Services ran a twice weekly service between Cardington and Shrewsbury (Barker Street), and working this service in August 1964, standing alongside the SBG in the previous picture, is EUJ 832, a Duple-bodied Bedford OB that was new to the business in 1948. In the right background is Mid Wales Motorways' Sentinel STC 4/40 CEP 147.** *Brian Botley*

Above: **This is MOD 688, a Brush-bodied Bedford SB, about to leave Barker Street in Shrewsbury in August 1964. This bus was new in 1951 and was purchased by Williamson's Motorways in July 1961 from Midway of Crymych.** *Brian Botley*

Below: **Several variants of diesel engine were fitted to the Bedford SB, but all had six cylinders. In 1953 the Perkins R6 of 5.562 litres was offered in the SBO, and in 1957 that was superseded by Bedford's own 4.927-litre diesel engine as the SB1. This is WAW 502, a Duple-bodied Bedford SB1 new to G. Cooper & Sons in 1961.** *Brian Botley*

Right: **W. Hoggins & Sons of Wrockwardine Wood, using the fleet name 'Pilot', was a member of the Shropshire Omnibus Association and purchased this Duple Midland-bodied Bedford SB5, 1194 NT, new in 1963. This view was taken in July 1964, and I believe that Hoggins had by this time sold the business to G. Cooper & Sons.** *Brian Botley*

Centre: **Williams Coachways, also of Wrockwardine Wood, was another member of the Shropshire Omnibus Association. This is HBW 306, a Duple-bodied Bedford SBG that was new in 1954 and was purchased by Williams from Unsworth of Wigan in June 1959. This view in Victoria Street, Wellington, dates from August 1964.** *Brian Botley*

Below right: **The Shropshire Omnibus Association's Donnington service benefited from the new Central Ordnance Depot, built by the Army in the 1930s, which had moved here from Woolwich Arsenal, and much associated housing was built for the workforce at the same time. Many of the runs on the route from Wellington terminated at the aptly named Garrison bus station. Standing at the bus stance in Victoria Street, Wellington, in August 1964 is UUJ 394, a Duple Midland-bodied Bedford SB1 that had been purchased new by A. Martlew & Sons in 1960.** *Brian Botley*

Above: T. G. Smith of Trench commenced operating in the 1920s, and by the time this view was taken in Wellington in August 1964 the business was known as Smith's Eagle Coachways Ltd. During the early and mid-1950s Burlingham produced a service bus body that had a simple outline but generally came with the brightwork motif on the front and with optional chrome trim strips along the sides. An example of this bodywork is seen here on NUX 256, an AEC Reliance, which was purchased new by Eagle in 1956. *Brian Botley*

Below: T. J. Green, trading as Worthen Motorways, took over some operations from Mid Wales Motorways in October 1963. Included in this take-over were four buses, which included CEP 264, a Churchill-bodied Commer Avenger I, which was new in 1951. The bus is seen here in Barker Street, Shrewsbury, in August 1964. Churchill Constructors Ltd produced coach bodywork for Commer, Austin, Bedford, Albion and Daimler from its premises in Norwich. *Brian Botley*

Right: **The business of T. W. Lewis was established in 1947, but did not operate stage services until 1962, when the services of W. H. Hailstone of Church Stoke, near Montgomery, were acquired. Working the Church Stoke to Shrewsbury service in August 1964 is NUN 167, a Burlingham-bodied Bedford SBG that had been new in 1956, and was purchased by Lewis's from Phillips of Rhostyllen in January 1962.** *Brian Botley*

Below: **Working the Shrewsbury to Wellington service in August 1964 is JAW 159, a Duple-bodied Bedford SB that was purchased new by Williamson's Motorways in 1952.** *Brian Botley*

Above: **Three days a week Williamson's Motorways had a service between Shrewsbury and Pulverbatch. Working this service in August 1964 is EUX 359, a Longford-bodied Bedford OB that was new in 1948. Neath & Cardiff bodied its own vehicles in 1937 and 1938, and in 1948 the company formed the Longford Manufacturing & Coachbuilders Co Ltd. Although only a short-lived venture, ceasing in 1953, it produced many pleasing and distinctive body styles.** *Brian Botley*

Below: **C. H. Butter of Yew Tree Cottage in Child's Ercall, between Telford and Market Drayton, ran a number of services in the Market Drayton area. Working a schools run in September 1964 is 448 GRE, one of a pair of Duple-bodied Bedford SBOs that had been new in 1955 and were purchased by Butter's from Greatrex of Stafford.** *Brian Botley*

Vaggs Motors of Knockin Heath, south of Oswestry, ran a pair of ex-City of Oxford Weymann-bodied AEC Regent IIIs, UWL 938 and UWL 940, that had been bought to replace the all-Leyland PD2s that had come new to the firm; I believe they arrived during the summer of 1968. The colour photograph shows UWL 940 shortly after being purchased, while in the other view we see it after having received Vaggs' livery of red, dark green and cream. The buses in the background are Strachan-bodied Dennis P5 Falcons, a number of which were purchased by Vaggs. *Brian Botley/Mark Hampson collection*

Between 1947 and 1953 Crosville was a regular purchaser of Bedford OBs, most of which were new. However, they had relatively short working lives with Crosville and the last were withdrawn in early 1960. Vaggs purchased a number of Crosville's Duple-bodied OBs in March 1960, including KFM 429 and KFM 430, seen in these two views. *Brian Botley/Mark Hampson collection*

Above: **Another of the buses acquired by Worthen Motorways from Mid Wales Motorways in October 1963 was this Duple-bodied Bedford OB, AEP 551, which was new in 1948. This view was taken at Barker Street in Shrewsbury in August 1964. The two-tone car in the left background is a Rover P4, which was widely known as the 'poor man's Rolls-Royce' and was rich in quality with an African walnut dash and window surrounds, coupled with a sumptuous leather interior.** *Brian Botley*

Right: **Salopia Coaches was started in the 1920s and became a limited company in March 1938. In the post-war years the company expanded rapidly in both stage services and long-distance tours. In 1962 it purchased four Duple Midland bus-bodied Bedford** SB1s, registered YAW 164 to 167, and representing this batch in this August 1964 view is the first of them. When just over eight years old, this bus was purchased by Sargent's of Kington, and remained with that company for three years. *Brian Botley*

Above: **Liverpool Corporation purchased four Duple-bodied Bedford OBs from BEA in 1952. In October 1961 Vaggs acquired one of them, UMY 96, and this view of it was taken at Vaggs' depot in September 1964.** *Brian Botley*

Below: **Heading for Maesbury in September 1964 is FUJ 564, a Mulliner-bodied Bedford OB that was new to Vaggs in 1949. I believe that the Mulliner coach/bus bodywork was completed in Birmingham. Mulliner's main business was specialist bodywork for cars and ambulances, and the building of bus and coach bodies ceased in 1958.** *Brian Botley*

Between April and June 1957 four ECW-bodied Bristol SC4LKs entered service with Eastern National as Nos 424 to 427 (601 to 604 JPU). By April 1964 they had been sold to and entered service with Vaggs. The first view of 603 JPU was taken in August 1964, and the colour view was taken in the summer of 1971. All four buses were withdrawn by Vaggs in November 1972. *Brian Botley/Mark Hampson collection*

Above: In May 1951 London Transport's RF 12 and RF 13 (LUC 212 and 213) entered service from Camberwell and Streatham depots respectively. They were part of the first batch of 25 Metro-Cammell-bodied AEC Regal IVs intended for private hire during the Festival of Britain, and were quite distinctive as they were only 27ft 6in long, and had glazed panels in the sides of the roof. Both buses were sold to PVS of Ilford, and in January 1964 were purchased by Hampson of Oswestry for use on the company's town service. This is LUC 213 working the Oswestry town service in September 1964. *Brian Botley*

Below: Entering the Barker Street bus stance in Shrewsbury in August 1964 is another Mulliner-bodied Bedford OB, EP 9031, this one having been purchased new by Williamson's Motorways in 1949. *Brian Botley*

Above: **PCY 546 is a Park Royal-bodied AEC Reliance that was new in December 1957 to David Jones & Sons of Pantdu, Port Talbot, and I believe that it did not last very long with that company. Jones operated a stage service in the Port Talbot area, together with the usual contract workings; the business passed to Thomas Bros (Port Talbot) Ltd in 1965, but none of the vehicles were taken over. Smith's Eagle purchased PCY 546 from Silvey of Eyney in June 1963, and it is seen here in Victoria Street, Wellington, in August 1964 working a Shropshire Omnibus Association rota service to Donnington.** *Brian Botley*

Below: **During 1963 Valley Motors purchased two new Duple-bodied Ford 570Es, 7901 and 7902 AW. This is the second of them at Barker Street, Shrewsbury, in August 1964. The excellent-looking car on the left is a Vauxhall PA, which was produced between 1957 and 1962.** *Brian Botley*

Above: **Worthen Motorways took over two Churchill-bodied Commer Avenger 1s from Mid Wales Motorways in October 1963, and this is the older of the two, CEP 168, new in 1951 and also seen here at Barker Street in August 1964.** *Brian Botley*

Below: **The first Sentinel models were the STC4, a lightweight integral product with bodywork by Sentinel to a Beadle design, and the SLC4, which was supplied as a chassis for outside bodying as bus or coach; most were bodied as coaches by Beadle. Six-cylinder-engined models followed, the STC6 and SLC6, but early problems with the engines and their mountings led to the company giving up on road vehicles in 1956. With the exception of Ribble, which bought 20, most purchasers were small independents, the best-known being Brown's of Donnington Wood. This is JUJ 264, an all-Sentinel STC new as a demonstrator in 1952. The bus was purchased by Brown's in April 1953 and is seen in Victoria Street, Wellington, in September 1964.** *Brian Botley*

Right: **During 1952 North Western Road Car took delivery of 10 all-Leyland PSU1/15s, FDB 600 to 609), but they lasted in the fleet for a relatively short period, all being withdrawn in 1961. One of the batch, FDB 605, was purchased by Jervis and entered service in August 1962. This view dates from 1964, by which time Jervis had sold his operations to Eagle.** *Brian Botley*

Centre: **J. E. Lowe & Sons of Trench was acquired by Smith's Eagle in July 1962, and one of the buses involved in the take-over was VTG 739, a Duple Midland-bodied Bedford SB8 that had been purchased new by Lowe in 1957. This view was taken in August 1964 in Wellington.** *Brian Botley*

Below right: **T. G. Smith, Eagle Coachways, purchased a number of heavyweight chassis, by AEC in particular, and in 1955 the business took delivery of a pair of 41-seat Burlingham Seagull coaches, LUJ 746 and 747, on AEC Reliance chassis. The first of the two, seen here in August 1964, left Smith's Eagle in May 1978, being sold together with the company's other old AECs – NUX 256, a Burlingham bus that had been bought new, and PCY 546, a Park Royal-bodied bus – to Smith of Ludlow, a scrap dealer, who sadly scrapped all three.** *Brian Botley*

During 1951 Brown's purchased a number of new Beadle coach-bodied Sentinel buses. The two seen here, HAW 303 and HAW 374, were photographed in April 1964. The end for the Brown's Sentinels came with the purchase on bus grant of new Bedford YRQs with Willowbrook bus bodies in 1971. *Brian Botley*

Above: **By 1954 the Shropshire Omnibus Association had seven operators listed on the Oakengates service (Cooper, Smith, Hoggins, Jervis, Jones, Price and Williams), so there were seven rotas a day, with four needed on Sundays. By 1966 there remained only four operators to Donnington and five to Oakengates, although by then there was a dominant operator on each route holding several shares, Cooper to Oakengates and Smith's Eagle to Donnington. This is Eagle Coachways' NNT 587, one of two Burlingham-bodied Bedford SBGs new to Eagle in 1957. The van behind is a new 1964 Ford Anglia.** *Brian Botley*

Above right: **The Bedford OWB was produced between 1942 and 1945, and more than 3,000 were built with a Duple-designed angular-shaped bodywork. The majority were built by Duple at Hendon, North London, although production was shared with Charles Roe of Crossgates, Leeds, SMT's Edinburgh workshops and Mulliner of Birmingham. OWBs were delivered in an overall semi-gloss dark brown finish, although many operators were able to source paints to produce their own individual liveries. The OWB was essentially a bus for the 'small operator', and was supplied in ones and twos according to need. This view of CAW 56, a Roe-bodied example new to Eagle in 1943, was taken in August 1964.** *Brian Botley*

Right: **Standing in Vaggs depot in the summer of 1970 is KNT 780, a Burlingham-bodied Leyland PSU1/15 that was new to Danny Gittins of Crickheath, Oswestry, in January 1954. It passed to Vaggs of Knockin Heath in April 1967, and remained in that fleet until the late 1970s, when it was rescued for preservation by the Vista Group in Hadnall. They sold the coach to Boulton's during 1987, which has continued the preservation of this good-looking coach.** *Brian Botley*

During 1959 Birch Brothers purchased a new Park Royal-bodied AEC Reliance, WLW 42; it was withdrawn from the company's fleet in 1969 and is seen here two years later when belonging to Vaggs. Also purchased by Vaggs from Birch Brothers in 1970 was YYX 43, a Duple-bodied AEC Reliance, which had been new to the Rushden firm in 1960. *Brian Botley*

Above: This is the only Leyland PSUC1/2 Tiger Cub to receive Yeates Europa bodywork, and was delivered new to Delaine's in 1958. After withdrawal the bus was sold to Vaggs, and this view of MTL 750 was taken in the summer of 1971. When Vaggs went out of business the bus was rescued by Delaine's and has been restored to that company's livery. *Brian Botley*

Below: Yelloway purchased seven new Harrington-bodied AEC Reliances between April and June 1962; registered 2921 to 2927 DK, they remained in the fleet until withdrawal during 1971 and 1972. One of them, 2923 DK, was purchased by Vaggs and is seen at the depot in July 1972. *Brian Botley*

Silver Service (Darley Dale)

Silver Service was the trading name of J. H. Woolliscroft & Son Ltd of Darley Dale, near Matlock, Derbyshire; the firm merged with Hulley's of Baslow in the 1970s, and the name Silver Service ceased to be used in the 1980s.

HTB 700 was an AEC Regal with a Trans-United coach body new to Kia Ora Motor Services Ltd, Morecambe, in July 1947. In October 1948 it passed to J. H. Woolliscroft as Silver Service No 16; it was withdrawn in November 1967, stored, then scrapped. Records would indicate that the chassis was new as FLM 386 in February 1939 with a Harrington coach body to A. Timpson & Sons, Catford, London SE6. During 1947 the chassis was rebuilt, fitted with an AEC 7.7-litre engine and rebodied by Trans-United Coach-Craft for Kia Ora. This view of the coach was taken at Matlock bus station in July 1960. *Brian Botley*

The first Harrington Wayfarer Mark 4 body appeared in time for the 1956 Commercial Motor Show, and was purchased in significant numbers; Maidstone & District took large batches, the last even after Cavalier production had started. In general, deliveries were no longer in ones and twos, with customers old and new buying fleets of 10 or more. The frontal appearance was simplified, with only two large windscreens rather than the fussy multi-pane of the previous model, and the curved glass for the main screen was discontinued. Legislation still required that the driver's windscreen should hinge open, and coaches and buses of all makes suffered many breakages as drivers tried to open their screens without properly unfastening them – at least flat glass meant that replacement was relatively cheap and easy. The large dummy grill was continued, but reshaped so that the headlamps were now outside it. The last coach made in this style was body 2546, registered PKP 120, delivered to Maidstone & District at the end of 1961. This is 149 UMP in July 1966, a Harrington Wayfarer Mark 4-bodied AEC Reliance, new to Gibson of Cockfosters in June 1959 and purchased by Silver Service in April 1960, remaining in the fleet until June 1974. *Brian Botley*

Above: By 1965 Strachan had largely dropped out of the PSV market, but made an attempt to re-enter it with the low-cost Pacesaver bodywork, which was initially designed for the Bedford SB chassis, and later the Bedford VAM. The bodywork was too utilitarian to attract even marginal operators and very few were sold for PSV use, although considerable numbers were taken by the Ministry of Defence on VAM chassis. In March 1965 Silver Service purchased two with Pacesaver bodywork on Bedford SB chassis, DRB 10C and 11C, and seen at Matlock bus station in August 1969 is the second of them. This bus was withdrawn from service in March 1972 and was later noted with Charcon Limited of Derby. *Mark Hampson collection*

Below: During 1961 Doncaster Corporation took delivery of six Roe-bodied AEC Reliances, 8625 to 8630 DT. They were all withdrawn in 1970 after a relatively short service life, and two of the batch, 8625 DT and 8629 DT, were acquired by Silver Service. This is 8625 DT, bought by Silver Service in September 1970, at Matlock bus station in September 1971. In September 1973 the bus was sold to Moseley of Shepshed and was acquired by Osborne's of Tollesbury for spares in November 1973. *Mark Hampson collection*

The Albion Nimbus was an underfloor-engined, ultra-lightweight bus or coach chassis, with a four-cylinder horizontal diesel engine and a gross vehicle weight of 6 tons, and was the first Albion bus chassis to have a name that did not begin with the letter V. It was largely operated on light rural bus duties and private hires – operators who used it on heavy-duty bus routes found it insufficiently robust. The design was revised twice and was produced from 1955 until 1965. In 1960, together with the rest of the Claymore range, the Nimbus was uprated, featuring heavier BMC axles and an Albion constant-mesh gearbox with either five or six speeds. Vacuum assistance to the brakes was now provided by a Hydrovac system, belt-driven from the engine. Two specific Nimbus changes were options of a drop-frame extension at the rear for a luggage boot, and a spare wheel mounted on a slide-out carrier below this extension. Nimbus production

amounted to 124 MR9s and 217 NS3s, and the largest user was Western Welsh, which kept them to deeply rural routes. Although operators using the Nimbus on intensive one-person-operated routes found it troublesome, on the lightly trafficked rural routes for which it was designed it could put in a long life. The Nimbus was nippy and economical, 11 to 12 miles per gallon, but the heavy town centre route was no place for it.

Halifax Joint Omnibus Committee purchased 10 NS3ANs, RJX 250 to 259, in May and June 1963, but they did not last long and all had been withdrawn by 1967. This is RJX 252, acquired by Silver Service in January 1967, at Crich in August 1969. It was withdrawn in June 1974 and sold to Schofield of Bury, which did not operate it; in December 1974 it was noted with Tottington Secondary School.

This is Silver Service No 23 (TCP 900), an AEC Reliance 2U3RA with an Alexander Y-type C49F body, parked at the company's Darley Dale depot on 9 July 1973. It was one of two purchased new in May 1964 by Hebble with bald dome, extra side flashes and originally a single-piece door. Numbered 73 and 74 in the Hebble fleet, they were renumbered 573 and 574 in 1970 and both were withdrawn by October 1972. This one was acquired by Silver Service in November 1972 and withdrawn in April 1976; it was at North's of Sherburn in May of that year.

Skill's (Nottingham)

Arthur Skill founded the firm in Radford in 1919, and by using his only lorry launched his first passenger service in that year. He used the same lorry to carry miners to Bestwood Colliery, and in 1921 he bought a Crossley charabanc, the company's first true bus. By 1927 he had introduced services to Bridlington and Scarborough, and later to Mablethorpe, Skegness, Cleethorpes and Southend-on-Sea. The purchase of other operators at various times added colliery services to Bilsthorpe and Gedling, and stage carriage services to East Bridgford and Bestwood. The trading arm of Skill's Motor Coaches became a limited company in 1958, and continental tours were introduced in the late 1970s.

Right: During 1952 Skill's purchased three new buses, a Willowbrook-bodied Leyland PSU1/15, a Duple-bodied Bedford SB, and, seen here, a Willowbrook-bodied AEC Regal IV (NAU 282), new in September of that year. This view was taken in November 1963, and just a few months later the bus was withdrawn and sold to Porthcawl Omnibus Co. By February 1966 it was in the fleet of Jenkins Tours of Llanelli, remaining there until 1974.

Above: Ribble Motor Services took delivery of large numbers of Leyland PD2/3s between 1948 and 1951, the majority of which were bodied by Leyland. This is ex-Ribble No 2653 (CCK 825), an all-Leyland PD2/3 new to Ribble in April 1949 and on that company's fleet strength until May 1963. Cowley of Salford acquired the bus that month, and in the same month Skill's purchased it. This view of CCK 825 was taken in November 1963, and it remained in the Skill's fleet until September 1965.

Working the Skill's Nottingham to East Bridgford service in November 1960 is 780 DAU, a Metro-Cammell-bodied Leyland PD3/1 that had been new to Skill's in March 1959. This bus passed to OK Motor Services in September 1970 and was acquired by Barratt, the building firm, in April 1973. By January 1976 it was in the fleet of Jopling Brothers of Birtley, but was lying derelict at that company's premises by December 1979.
Brian Botley

South Notts

Bottom left and right:
The South Notts single-deckers in general operated the Nottingham to Kegworth village service, which had a number of narrow roads and tight bends. Many were short workings to Barton-in-Fabis or Thrumpton, and others included West Leake or Kingston-on-Soar if it was a market day. This is therefore an unusual view of MRR 974, an all-Leyland PSU1/11 new to South Notts in March 1952, indicating route 61A to Clifton Estate. Standing behind it in this July 1970 view is CCK 648, a Brush-bodied Leyland PD2/3 new to Ribble in 1949 and acquired by South Notts in February 1961, remaining in the fleet until February 1972. The second picture shows a more usual allocation of MRR 974, waiting to take up a journey to Thrumpton. *Mark Hampson collection/Brian Botley*

Below: **As the Clifton Estate expanded more Clifton services were introduced in 1955, and during May and June of that year South Notts took delivery of two Weymann-bodied Leyland PD2/20s, RRR 912 and 913). This view of RRR 912 was taken at Gotham depot in November 1971. If you look carefully, framed neatly by the washing equipment in the background is MAL 310, a Duple-bodied Leyland Royal Tiger PSU1/11, which was new to South Notts in 1951 and had just been withdrawn from service when this picture was taken.** *Brian Botley*

Above: During 1957 South Notts added four coaches to its fleet; two were Duple-bodied Leyland PSU1/15s, acquired from Jackson of Castle Bromwich, and one was a Bedford OB, purchased from Barton. The only new coach purchased that year was XAL 239, a Duple Donington-bodied Leyland PSUC1/2 that arrived in July 1957. This view was taken in September 1965. *Brian Botley*

Below: The first new double-decker, 76 LNN, with Northern Counties bodywork, was delivered in October 1961 and is seen here in Nottingham in July 1967. This bodybuilder was to feature in all but two of the double-decker purchases from 1960 to 1991.

From September 1963 until March 1967, South Notts purchased five new Northern Counties-bodied Albion LR3 Lowlanders. This is the second of them, 84 WRR, new in May 1964 and seen at Huntingdon Street bus station, Nottingham, in October 1964. The Huntingdon Street stands were in two parts, best described as the northern and southern halves; the southern half has been completely built over and is now a Staples office store. The second view of 84 WRR was taken in the summer of 1977. *Brian Botley/Mark Hampson collection*

Above: **Bedford coaches were regularly purchased by South Notts, including the Bedford SB5; the last new one was CRR 86C, bodied by Duple and delivered in May 1965. This view was taken in the late summer of 1970, and the coach remained in the fleet until September 1977, when it was acquired by Bird of Hunstanton.** *Mark Hampson collection*

Below and above right: **In November 1968 South Notts took delivery of its first rear-engine double-deck bus, TNN 90G, and five months later, in April 1969, two similar Northern Counties-bodied Leyland PDR1/3s were delivered. They were registered VAL 306G and 307G, and seen in the first photograph** *(below)*, **when new and working**

the Loughborough service, is the second of them. The second picture (*above*) was taken in the winter of 1972. *Brian Botley/Mark Hampson collection*

Below: Two more Northern Counties-bodied Leyland PDR1/3s, DVO 96J and 97J, arrived in January 1971, and this view of DVO 96J is dated April 1971. These two buses were the last Leyland PDR1/3 chassis purchased by South Notts. *Brian Botley*

J. Stevenson (Uttoxeter)

It was in 1926 that John Stevenson sold his farm at Fole, near Uttoxeter, to buy two former US school buses and set up Stevenson's in Spath. A service was started between Uttoxeter and Beamhurst, and quite quickly two further routes were started. In November 1941 a limited company was formed, but the fleet remained licensed to John Stevenson until his death. The company later took over the licences, and by the early 1970s operated a number of services in the Uttoxeter, Ashbourne and Burton-upon-Trent areas.

During June 1949 RTL 270 (KGU 216), a Park Royal-bodied Leyland PD2/1, entered service with London transport at Tottenham garage on route 73. During January 1957 the bus was transferred to Walworth depot, and a month later was dispatched to Aldenham for overhaul. The following month it was transferred to Seven Kings depot, and remained there until it was stored at Lea Bridge in November 1958. Stevenson's purchased the bus and it entered service as No 29 in November 1959. It is seen here, complete with well-dented roof, in December 1969.
Brian Botley

Above: **This is No 12 in the Stevenson's fleet, 4799 RF, a Duple-bodied Ford 570E that was purchased new in 1960 and entered service in June of that year. This view was taken in December 1969.** *Brian Botley*

Below: **Blue Line (Samuel Morgan Ltd) of Armthorpe, near Doncaster, was a loyal customer of Guy Motors of Wolverhampton,** taking new and second-hand examples from 1943 until 1967. In 1956 Blue Line acquired RWT 613, a Burlingham-bodied Guy Arab UF; it was later acquired by Stevenson's, given the fleet number 1, and entered service in January 1964. Standing next to it is another Guy, RRF 773, this time an Arab III, new to Stevenson's as No 3 in May 1949. This picture was taken in August 1967. *Mark Hampson collection*

Above: **London Transport all-Leyland PD2/3 RTW 178 (KLB 908) entered service on route 112 from Palmers Green depot in December 1949. Between May and July 1950 the bus was used for width tests at Middle Row and Hackney depots. From March 1951 until May 1957 it operated from Clay Hall depot, then Hackney. After overhaul at Aldenham, RTW 178 operated from Dalston and Putney depots until it was stored in May 1965. Purchased by Bird's of Stratford-upon-Avon, a month later the bus was quickly acquired by Stevenson's and fitted with platform doors, remaining in** the fleet until late 1975. This view of No 11 was taken in March 1973. *Brian Botley*

Below: **Between February and September 1959 Yorkshire Woollen District took delivery of 22 AEC Reliances; 14 had Park Royal bodywork and the remaining eight had bodywork finished by Roe. Two were purchased by Stevenson's from Smythe of London and entered service as Nos 7 and 26 (DHD 193 and DHD 192) in November and December 1970. This view of No 7 was taken in May 1971.** *Brian Botley*

Above: The very first Leyland L1s were delivered to Sheffield Joint Omnibus Committee in July 1959 and had Weymann Fanfare coach bodywork; they were in fact delivered before the model was officially launched at the Scottish Motor Show in November of that year. The six, 1500 to 1505 WJ, were originally described as Leyland PSUC1 Specials, but on delivery this had been changed to L1 Leyland. A further five L1s with Fanfare bodywork were purchased by Sheffield in 1960, and Stevenson's subsequently purchased three of the coaches, 1500 WJ, 1501 WJ and 1914 WA. This is No 1 (1501 WJ), which entered service in August 1971. *Mark Hampson collection*

Below: Sheffield Joint Omnibus Committee and Sheffield Railway took delivery of nine Burlingham dual-purpose-bodied Leyland L1s in 1960. Five went to the Sheffield Railway fleet, and two of those that went to the JOC were later purchased by Stevenson's; this is No 18 (5907 W), which entered service in May 1972 and is seen here in the early winter of that year. *Brian Botley*

During the early 1970s Stevenson's also purchased three double-deck buses from Sheffield, and one of these was 6349 WJ, a Roe-bodied AEC Regent V, seen in this December 1972 view without a fleet number at that time. Together with many more in the fleet, this bus was fitted with platform doors and entered service in November 1972. On the left is No 8 (966 CWL), which was reseated to H41/32 with rear doors prior to entering service in February 1970. This bus was originally City of Oxford No 966 and was new in 1958. On the right is No 30 (EHE 160), a Roe-bodied Leyland PSU1/13 that had been new to Yorkshire Traction in 1951 and was already nearly 16

years old when acquired by Stevenson's in early 1967. *Mark Hampson collection*

W. Stonier & Sons

The business began by operating excursions from May 1919, and it was not until the late 1920s that service operations commenced. A limited company was formed in 1937, at which time the fleet was quite small. An significant increase in vehicle numbers only began in the late 1950s when services, jointly with Potteries Motor Traction, began in the Bentilee area.

Hants & Sussex purchased 10 Leyland PD1s in 1947, seven with NCB bodywork and three by Leyland. In January 1955 Stonier's acquired two of them, FCG 523 and FCG 525, both with NCB bodywork, and this wonderful view shows FCG 523 in

September 1959, just a few months before its withdrawal from service. *Brian Botley*

Above: **Stonier's purchased three Duple-bodied Bedford SB3s from Salopia Saloon Coaches Ltd of Whitchurch. They were registered UNT 131, new in 1960, and WNT 252 and WNT 257, new in 1961; the first, UNT 131, arrived in March 1962, the others arriving in April 1963. This is WNT 257, which appears to be smoking excessively from its six-cylinder 4.927-litre Bedford petrol engine; this managed only 7 miles per gallon, whereas the Bedford diesel engine managed up to 18. This bus was withdrawn from service in August 1970 and scrapped.** *Brian Botley*

Below: **Ribble purchased 110 all-Leyland PSU1/13 Royal Tigers in late 1951 and 1952. The body was of standard Leyland metal-frame construction with 44 seats. A major modification to the Leyland standard design was the repositioning of the front entrance, which was as far forward as possible to allow maximum knee-room for the seats. Another departure from the Leyland standard design was the windscreen, which had the maximum possible inclination from the vertical to improve driver visibility in adverse driving conditions. Ribble No 366 (ERN 689) was withdrawn by Ribble in April 1964 and purchased by Stonier's. It was numbered 5 in the fleet, and is looking quite smart in this December 1968 view. No 5 was withdrawn in May 1969 and purchased by Harper Brothers of Heath Hayes for spares.** *Brian Botley*

Above: **By mid-1965 Hutchison's Coaches (Overtown) Ltd had only three double-deck buses in its fleet. The first to be withdrawn and sold was LVA 483, a 1955 Northern Counties-bodied Leyland PD2/12, which was purchased by Stonier's in August 1965. This view of No 7 was taken at the Goldenhill depot in December 1968. No 5 (ERN 689) can be seen in the background.** *Brian Botley*

Below: **The second ex-Hutchison's bus to be purchased arrived in November 1965; registered KVA 511, it was given fleet number 8. It was an all-Leyland PD2/12 new in 1954, and is in service to Bentilee in this January 1967 view. This bus was withdrawn from service in June 1972 and noted at Hughes, a dealer, in July 1972.** *Brian Botley*

Above: **The last former Hutchison's bus to enter service, in June 1966, was RVA 763, a Northern Counties-bodied Leyland PD2/30 that had been new in 1958. No 4 is exiting Hanley bus station for Mere in January 1970.**

Right: **J. Laurie & Co of Burnbank, Hamilton, which traded under the name 'Chieftain', was acquired by Central SMT in 1961. The purchased fleet contained a number of ex-London Leyland Titans and a few bought new by Laurie, Leyland PD2s and Leyland PD3s. This is PVD 629, No 2 in the Stonier's fleet, in January 1970. A Northern Counties-bodied Leyland PD3/1, it had been new to Laurie's in 1957 and was purchased by Stonier's from Central SMT in October 1967, remaining in service until October 1971.**

Above: **On 31 March 1968 the Wallace Arnold group sold Kippax & District Motor Co to Leeds Corporation, together with its near neighbour the Farsley Omnibus Company. Between 1960 and 1965 Kippax had purchased new four Leyland PD3s – 6237 UB, 556 DUA, DUG 166C and DUG 167C – and in April 1968 Stonier's purchased 556 DUA. It was numbered 10 and is seen leaving Hanley bus station for the journey to Bentilee in May 1970. The bus on the extreme right is one of Procter's Alexander-bodied Daimler CRG's, No 10, which survived in the fleet until late 1979.**

Right: **Yorkshire Woollen District took delivery of a large batch of Metro-Cammell-bodied AEC Regent Vs during 1958. During 1969 seven** of them, DHD 184 to 190, were transferred to Hebble, then in late 1970 DHD 184 was withdrawn from service and by January 1971 had been purchased by Stonier's. This view of No 1 was taken at Goldenhill depot in the winter of 1972. *Mark Hampson collection*

Above: **In September 1962 Turner's of Brown Edge purchased new a Massey-bodied Leyland PD3/4, 961 GBF; it remained in Turner's fleet until March 1971, when it was purchased by Stonier's. The bus is reversing out of a stance at Hanley bus station in February 1974.**

Below: **Between October and December 1971 Stonier's purchased from the City of Oxford fleet 301 KFC and 302 KFC, East Lancs-bodied Dennis Lolines that had been new in 1960.**

They were as much oddities in the Stonier's fleet as they had been in their home town, and their AEC AV470 engines were not best suited to hilly North Staffordshire; they particularly did not like Limekiln Bank on the main route in from Bentilee to Hanley. This view of No 5 (302 KFC) was taken in February 1974; within a few months both Lolines had been withdrawn from service, and 301 KFC was noted with Cobholm Coaches in September 1974, still with its Stonier's fleet number 6.

S. Turner & Sons (Brown Edge)

S. Turner began operations in 1922 with a Ford T, and the fleet remained small until 1951, when the first double-deck buses were acquired form Salford Corporation. From 1957 the business began to purchase new buses, and a year later a limited company was formed.

The first new double-deck bus, purchased in 1957, was a Massey-bodied Leyland PD2/30. The next three were all also bodied by Massey, and this is No 6 (961 GBF), a Leyland PD3/4 that was new in September 1962, and is seen here at Hanley bus station in September 1968. Turner was well supported by the public, being known locally as 'Sammy's Buses', and the vehicles were always immaculately presented. *Brian Botley*

The first rear-engine bus purchased new by Turner was No 9 (BRF 733E), a Northern Counties-bodied Daimler CRG6 of January 1967. This view of No 9 was also taken at Hanley bus station, this time in September 1967. This bus subsequently passed to Morris Bros, Swansea, then to Leon of Finningley, by which time it had received a Leyland 680 engine. *Brian Botley*

Warrington (Ilam)

In the 1920s there were two bus operators in the small village of Ilam, near Ashbourne, Mr Warrington and Messrs Sellars & Kent. The latter sold out to Hulley's of Baslow, and the licences operated by Warrington's by 1970 were between Ilam and Leek and Ilam and Ashbourne.

Leaving Ashbourne on the journey to Ilam in December 1970 is KAB 984, a Duple-bodied Bedford SB that had been new to Don's of Bishop's Stortford in 1951. It was acquired by Warrington's in July 1962, and was still in the fleet in April 1973.

Warstone Motors
(Green Bus Service)

The first service operated by Warstone Motors of Great Wyrley commenced in the mid-1970s and was between Cannock and Penkridge. The first two buses acquired for this service were a Leyland Olympian and a Bedford OB. Services gradually expanded to Bishop's Wood and Telford, and the first double-deck bus, a Guy Arab, joined the fleet. In 1980 Warstone, now trading as Green Bus, became part of the 'Chaserider' scheme and operated between Cannock and Calf Heath, Wolverhampton and Landywood, and part of Wolverhampton to Brewood. In 1984, when Blue Bus Services ceased running, Green Bus ran regularly into Walsall.

About to set off on a Cannock local service to Longford Bridge in May 1979 is one of the first buses purchased by Warstone Motors, No 14 (521 CTF), a rare MCW-bodied Leyland Olympian that had been new to Fishwick's of Lancashire in 1957. *Mark Hampson collection*

Above: In January 1962 Rees & Williams purchased a Massey-bodied Guy Arab IV (YTH 815), which had a Johannesburg front. This bus became the first double-deck bus to be operated by Green Bus in 1977 and remained in the fleet until the early 1980s. Note the badly crushed roof panels, caused by low-hanging tree branches in the Staffordshire countryside, but still No 4 looks smart in this May 1979 view. *Mark Hampson collection*

Below: Green Bus owned three ex-Burnley & Colne Leyland Tiger Cubs, numbering them 1, 2, and 3 in its fleet. Despite being quite austere and notoriously difficult to drive, they lasted quite a number of years with the operator. This is No 3 (BCW 469B) with an East Lancashire body, new to Burnley & Colne in 1964, heading for Wolverhampton in June 1980. The blue car on the right is an Austin Princess, which was launched to critical acclaim on 26 March 1975 as the 18-22 Series, 'the car that has got it all together'. Like many other controversial cars, the exterior styling was distinctive. 'The Wedge', as it was often nicknamed, was indeed very wedge-shaped and the styling was all angles and slanting panels. Unfortunately the Princess was affected by poor build quality and constant industrial disputes, and it gained a reputation for unreliability that it could never shake off, even though quality improved in later years. The styling, praised upon introduction, was soon labelled 'ugly', and it was suggested that the people responsible for designing the front and rear of the car had not been speaking to one another. *Mark Hampson collection*

Caerphilly Urban District Council took delivery of three Massey-bodied Leyland PD3/4s in late 1965, and all three subsequently passed to Rhymney Valley District Council. One of them became Green Bus Service No 12 (GNY 432C), and it is seen in the first picture working route 10 to Wolverhampton in the summer sun of 1980. The yellow car behind it is a Triumph Toledo. The second view was taken less than a month later. *Mark Hampson collection/Brian Botley*

Among the last Leyland Titans to be built were a batch of PD3/4s that were new to Stockport during January and February 1969. One of this batch was No 92 (MJA 892G), and this became No 5892 in the fleet of SELNEC in November 1969. When Green Bus acquired the bus it became No 8 and, as seen in this August 1984 view in Cannock, the company decided to repaint its lovely old ex-Stockport Corporation bus from its fine green and yellow livery into a garish two-tone green and cream. Not surprisingly, the livery was short-lived and the bus was painted back into standard fleet livery shortly afterwards, as shown in the second picture. *Brian Botley/Mark Hampson collection*

Bradford Corporation purchased 15 Neepsend-bodied Leyland PD3A/2s during 1967, numbered 241 to 255 (FKY 241E to 255E), and they survived to become part of the West Yorkshire Passenger Transport Executive fleet with the same numbers. This is FKY 244E as No 20 in the Green Bus Service fleet in the summer of 1984; however, it lasted for a very short time before being withdrawn and sold on. *Mark Hampson collection*

E. Webster & Sons (Hognaston)

E. Webster & Sons ran a small coach business from the village of Hognaston in Derbyshire, which also operated a service between Ashbourne and Derby, and had a timetable built around the needs of a rural community. A regular performer on the service would be a Bedford OB with one of Mr Webster's daughters as the conductress.

This is Brassington in December 1970, and on its way to Ashbourne is MTB 533, a Duple Vista-bodied Bedford OB that had been new in 1950 and was acquired by Webster's from Gleave of Audlem in 1954.

This view was also taken in Brassington on the same day, and this is Webster's 887 R, a Bedford SB5 with Duple Bella Vega bodywork purchased new in 1963. It is awaiting departure for Derby – note the small destination blind on the bumper.

Worth's Motor Services (Enstone)

The 11th-built AEC Reliance with Duple Elizabethan bodywork, new to Creamline of Bordon in 1954, was MOU 454. This view, taken at the parking area at Gloucester Green bus station in Oxford in May 1965, shows the bus in the livery of Worth's of Enstone. *Brian Botley*

Yorkshire Woollen District purchased 22 Park Royal-bodied AEC Reliances (DHD 191 to 213) between February and September 1959, and eight of them were completed by Roe on Park Royal frames. This picture of DHD 195, now in the fleet of Worth's, was also taken at Gloucester Green bus station, in July 1970, by which time the parking area had been resurfaced. *Brian Botley*

York Brothers (Northampton)

In 1924 Mr George York purchased a Model T Ford and developed his own carrier and passenger service in Cogenhoe, Northampton. The vehicle, which was used to carry coal most of the time, had a detachable top and was used to take passengers from Cogenhoe to Northampton on market days. In 1925 another Model T Ford was purchased, and in 1926 a Chevrolet. In that year George York was joined by his brother Fred, who left his business as a blacksmith in Ravenstone, Buckinghamshire. The firm grew gradually throughout the 1920s, and in 1928 the bus service was extended to Wollaston, and a Summer express service

from Northampton to Great Yarmouth began. During the 1920s the York brothers moved their business to new premises in the village, now the Cogenhoe Garage of Mixconcrete Transport Ltd.

In about 1930 York Brothers moved to Northampton, renting a garage in Dychurch Lane, off Abington Street, at the rear of the Black Boy Hotel (later the Midland Bank), and a few years later they also rented a garage at West Bridge, St James's End, Northampton. The first coach ticket booking office opened in Derngate in 1932.

During the 1930s the coach fleet was expanded with purchases of Maudslay vehicles and, in 1937, Leylands. In 1940 all but one of York Brothers' 15 coaches were commandeered for the transport of troops, although the local stage carriage bus service continued, using the remaining coach and one old spare vehicle. After the Coventry Blitz, the company purchased coaches to ferry workers from Northampton to the rebuilt Coventry munitions factories. Also in the 1940s a garage at South Bridge, Northampton, was acquired.

In 1946 George York ceased to be actively involved in the company, going into farming at Church Farm, Little Houghton. Fred York and his son Alfred, who later became Managing Director, continued to run the company, while Fred's other son, Robert, became the chief maintenance engineer.

The company continued to expand during the 1950s. In 1951 York Brothers opened a booking office in Market Street, Kettering, and rented a garage in London Road. In 1957/58 the booking office moved to Tanners Lane, and in 1975 to High Street, Kettering. In about 1958 York Brothers took over Seamark's Motors Ltd of Rushden and opened its own garage and booking office there. In 1956 a garage was also opened at Barker's Yard, Wellingborough. Since that time more booking offices have been opened, at Wellingborough in 1967/68, in the Weston Favell Centre in Northampton in 1975, and in the Grosvenor Centre, Northampton, in 1976. Several smaller coach companies have also been taken over, including Law's Coaches in 1930, Abbott's Coaches of Wellingborough in about 1962, and Knight's of Kingsthorpe Grove, Northampton, in 1963. York Brothers continued its local bus service until 1976, when it was sold to United Counties.

Duple's Britannia body was introduced in 1955, based on the Elizabethan but with vertical pillars. In 1957 York Brothers purchased an **AEC Reliance with this bodywork, No 70 (ORP 600), this view being taken in September 1965.**

Above: **On an excursion in Kidderminster in July 1966 is No 81 (YRD 81), one of two Duple Britannia-bodied AEC Reliances that were new to York Brothers in May 1961.**

Below: **During April 1966 York Brothers took delivery of a Duple Northern Commander-bodied AEC Reliance, No 88 (GNV 88D), and this view of the bus was taken during its first season of tours in the summer of 1966, this one destined for Yarmouth.**

THE BRITISH BUSES, TRAMS and TROLLEYBUSES SERIES
from
The NOSTALGIA Collection
It's not just about looking back!

Part 1: THE MIDLANDS

238 x 172mm	128pp	c240 ill
ISBN 978 1 85794 341 2	Softcover	£17.99

Part 2: SOUTH WALES

238 x 172mm	128pp	c240 ill
ISBN 978 1 85794 342 9	Softcover	£17.99

Part 3: THE SOUTH WEST

238 x 172mm	128pp	c220 ill
ISBN 978 1 85794 368 9	Softcover	£17.99

Part 4: THE NORTH EAST, EAST YORKSHIRE & DURHAM

238 x 172mm	128pp	c240 ill
ISBN 978 1 85794 359 7	Softcover	£17.99

Part 5: SOUTH, WEST & NORTH YORKSHIRE

238 x 172mm	128pp	c240 ill
ISBN 978 1 85794 385 6	Softcover	£17.99

Part 6: LONDON AREA & THE SOUTH EAST COAST

238 x 172mm	128pp	c240 ill
ISBN 978 1 85794 387 0	Softcover	£17.99

Part 7: SOUTH EAST & EAST ANGLIA

238 x 172mm	128pp	c240 ill
ISBN 978 1 85794 388 7	Softcover	£17.99

Part 8: NORTH WALES TO MERSEYSIDE including the ISLE OF MAN

238 x 172mm	128pp	c220 ill
ISBN + 394 8	Softcover	£18.00

Part 9: GREATER MANCHESTER, LANCASHIRE AND CUMBRIA

238 x 172mm	128pp	c220 ill
ISBN 978 1 85794 397 9	Softcover	£18.00

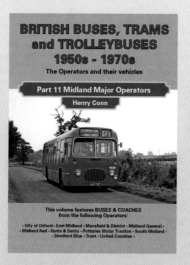

Part 11: MIDLAND MAJOR OPERATORS

The more than 200 photographs in this new volume in the series were taken between 1951 and 1978. The majority are in colour and have never before been published. Covering all the major bus, tram and trolleybus operators in the area, most of the pictures show the buses in pre-National Bus Company and Passenger Transport Executive liveries. They also, of course, provide nostalgic views of street scenes, shops and contemporary road vehicles.

Midlands Major Operators will feature buses and coaches of:
City of Oxford
East Midland
Mansfield & District
Midland General
Midland Red
Notts & Derby
Potteries Motor Traction
South Midland
Stratford Blue
Trent
United Counties

Part 10: MIDLAND INDEPENDENT OPERATORS

238 x 172mm	128pp	c240 ill
ISBN 978 1 85794 397 9	Softcover	£18.00

Part 11: MIDLAND MAJOR OPERATORS

238 x 172mm	128pp	c200 ill
ISBN 978 1 85794 397 9	Softcover	£18.00

Further Reading For Road Transport Enthusiasts
from
The NOSTALGIA Collection
it's not just about looking back!

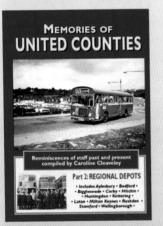

Memories of UNITED COUNTIES

The first two volumes of this series, published by Silver Link Publishing and covering Northampton – the United Counties headquarters, the principal bus station at Derngate, and the works at Bedford Road and Rothersthorpe Avenue – and the regional depots – from Aylesbury to Wellingborough – struck such a chord in former employees that further reminiscences were triggered, and they are included in the third volume, almost a 'supplement' to the other two.

Like all large service organisations, bus companies present a very familiar, everyday face to the public at large, but are fascinatingly complex beneath the surface, and it is the intricacies of providing an efficient bus service that are revealed by these varied staff memories. Principal among them are stories of working lives with United Counties at Bedford, Luton and Wellingborough, with fascinating extracts from the Rushden Depot Minute Book covering the years 1950 to 1963.

Northampton-born Caroline Cleaveley has been fascinated by United Counties and its family of employees since childhood, when as a youngster she unofficially assisted friendly conductors and paid regular visits to the works. She now lives in Gloucestershire and is the owner of an old Huntingdon-based United Counties bus that had migrated away to Luton many years ago.

Part 3 is a limited run and has been produced on behalf of Caroline Cleaveley by *Priory Ash Publishing*.

Silver Link is pleased to make this third volume available to our customers while stocks last.

Memories of United Counties Vol 1		
ISBN 978 1 85794 343 6	Softcover	£17.99

Memories of United Counties Vol 2		
ISBN 978 1 85794 344 3	Softcover	£19.99

Memories of United Counties Vol 3		
ISBN 978 1 85794 871 7	Softcover	£10.00